CONVERTING CUSTOMERS TO CLIENTS

A Guide to Strengthen Your Business Relationships

CHRIS WENDEL

Author and Entrepreneur

CONVERTING CUSTOMERS TO CLIENTS

A Guide to Strengthen Your Business Relationships

§

CHRIS WENDEL

HP

HOLDEN PUBLISHING

ALL BOOKS BY CHRIS WENDEL

Novels
Human After All

Short Stories
Human After All: The Pen Pal Chronicle
(An Amazon Bestseller)

Business Books
Converting Customers to Clients
On Strengthening Business Relationships

Cover design by: Chris Wendel
Cover Art Work by: 3DStock

ISBN: 978-0-9895714-0-1
e-ISBN: 978-0-9895714-1-8

Acknowledgements

I'd like to thank the following people for their tireless support during the writing of this book, as well as their amazing critiques: Bart Ross, John Wentworth, David Wendel, Joyce Wendel, Bill Wendel, Donna Torres, Bryan Wendel, Michelle Wendel, Peggy Wendel, Mary Wendel, the rest of my family, and Karen Hudson.

Thank you to John F. Wendel for being a trusted advisor through every step of my business transactions. Thank you to Al Wendel for being a great example of hard work combined with fairness and niceness.

Additionally, thanks to Nikki Barnes and Mark Dixon of Taylor and Andrew Photography for my jacket photographs. Brian Hall of Think Dual Brain for so much great web site, app, and marketing assistance.

Finally, thank you (1.) to Holly Geddie for buying into my version of Relationship Marketing and sticking with it for so many years, as well as for being an amazing assistant and friend (*we figured it out one day at a time, didn't we?*), and (2.) to all my clients: thank you for teaching me about myself, people, families, the world, and business.

-    CW

Dedication

To Holden Wendel

Embrace the positivity of being human. Take with you through your life's journey the world's wondrous opportunities to experience wholly your existence. My best to you always.

In Memoriam

David I. Wendel

For teaching me to care for the people I serve.

Ken Cassel

For your friendship, constant interest, and mentoring in all my business dealings, as well as sharing your infectious laugh with me.

Jim Lee

For your passion, friendship, philanthropy, advice, assistance, and continually making sure you were paying me enough. You were. More than you know.

Gene Gelb

My first boss and professional mentor, who spent equal amounts of time lovingly guiding me professionally and personally. Your lessons live on. Thanks.

Everyone has this desire for the authentic. Authenticity is, therefore, becoming the new consumer sensibility. The buying criteria by which consumers are choosing who they are going to buy from and what they are going to buy, becoming the basis of the economy.

There are two dimensions to authenticity. One, being true to yourself, which is very self-directed. Two, is other-directed. Being what you say you are, to others.

- Joseph Pine

Introduction

Your relationship with a client is as important as having a service to provide a client. Without one, you'll never survive the stormy waters of the small and medium business environment. I owned an IT consulting company in Florida for almost a decade. During that time, I was lucky enough to build relationships with the majority of my clients. I never claimed to be the best IT technician, but I think I was the best at building relationships.

I have listened to dozens of clients negatively describe their past experiences with other IT technicians, and each experience confounded me. I never have, and still don't, understand how independent IT consultants expect to stay in business and keep clients without providing premier service *and* building relationships. The two go hand-in-hand. One without the other doesn't work, yet so many businesses consistently either don't relate well with their clients or they provide terrible customer service. Worse, they don't do either well. I realized, by listening to those described experiences, how I could set myself apart from my competition. I continued to learn my trade and develop what I believed to be the best practices for building relationships with my clients. And, it worked! I have many relationships that are ongoing even though I have sold that business, which is something I am very proud to say.

If you're a professional service provider (IT consultant, CPA, attorney, marketing or branding expert, etc.), then your whole business is based on relationships. To that end, this book is dedicated to helping you initiate, build, and maintain a relationship with your clients. Yes, you have to be good at what you do, but you must be great at interacting, engaging, nurturing, and connecting with people. The ability to do so makes you either a tremendously valuable asset to your firm and/or a powerful threat to your business's competition.

Many professional service providers have notorious reputations/stereotypes for not being able to connect with people, not being able to communicate well with people, and not being able to ease people's concerns about their respective troubles. So, for those who have the natural ability to connect with people and build relationships, congratulations. For the rest of you, this book will help.

What Makes a Relationship?

It's generally accepted that relationships are founded in the following characteristics:

- Honesty
- Communication
- Care
- Respect
- Trust
- Commitment

Honest Communication leads to Caring and Respectful Trust, which then culminates in Commitment of service quality (on your part) and of continued service contracting (on your client's part). Therefore, every act of service quality must be founded in honesty, open communication, care, respect, trust, and commitment. Every interaction—every phone call, email, text, face-to-face occurrence (be it social or professional), invoice, report, social media post, every piece of marketing material, and even every word-of-mouth comment people make about you when you're not even present—needs to contain these six elements of relationships.

It may seem daunting, and I don't like using *absolute* words, like "every" or "always" or "never" or "none." I hesitate to use them because no one can do any one thing "always" or "never" (*Oops, I did it!*). How can you foster this type of consistency?

By changing.

Read the Core Principles in this book. I believe if you change how you view your job, yourself, and your clients, then you will change your understanding of how each is connected to the other; then the subsequent principles, philosophies, and ideas in the book should be easy to implement. Plus, you don't have to implement every idea in the book and certainly not all at once. The more you can implement, the better your relationships will mature. Find and focus on the ones that work best for your personality. Start by implementing three. Use them in the field with your clients and monitor the progress. Then implement ten. Keep that progression until you have all these philosophies as part of your professional personality.

Good luck!

Who Should Read This?

Originally, this book was aimed at the Information Technology industry because that's where my experience showed the biggest need for assistance in turning customers into fully humanized clients. However, after speaking with business owners in various professional service industries, I found a common desire for these providers to build relationships with their customers. I noticed a trend among the providers, consumers, and even advertisers for human connection, authentic interaction, and genuine exchanges. Yet more and more our society (through technological advances and economic limitations) is moving further away from this model; these advances and limitations are moving us away from our most basic commonality—being human.

So who should read this book?

Sole Proprietors. The sole proprietor is usually the entrepreneur and the technician. S/He is the subject matter expert and the business owner. S/He is the person running the business and the one performing the expert work for which the business is being paid. Without the sole proprietor, the company makes no money. The system of business is totally dependent on her/him.

Thus, a sole proprietor's day (every day) is jammed packed. So many issues can take their attention away from their work—family obligations, clients, vehicle problems, technology, accounting and legalities, management, scheduling and logistics, and continuing education, to name a few. The over-stressed sole proprietor can sometimes forget about connecting with her/his clients, preferring to rush through tasks and appointments simply to cross it off her/his list.

On good days, there may only be 20 things swirling inside a sole proprietor's mind. On bad days, there could be two or three dozen more things to worry about. It's easy to forget some aspects of the job, like connecting with clients. However, connecting with clients should be so ingrained that doing so is second nature. Especially for the sole proprietor, keeping and maintaining a client list is easier than continually finding new clients. If your services expand over time and your client list is happy with you and your product, then they'll expand with you. The only way to keep clients (notice I didn't use the word "customers") is to build a relationship.

Business Owners. These are men and women who own a business but by and large do not go out on calls to clients' offices and/or homes. Maybe they go on sales calls, but they don't perform the daily technical functions of their provided service. They have staff who interact regularly with clients (and other staff).

Business owners have a lot to worry about, and a great deal of that worry centers around staffing issues. How will staff members interact with clients? Will staff members injure themselves? Will vehicles come back to the office damaged? Will their technicians/staff get into situations that could be deemed inappropriate? People's definitions of appropriateness are as varied as the people themselves. An incident one person finds innocuous, another may find offensive. In this business setting, the business owner sets the scale of appropriateness, but then s/he has to trust his staff to act accordingly. S/He also has to trust the message of what is and isn't appropriate was communicated and received by staff members on a wavelength that was comprehensible. This book will help with that.

Maybe you already have a training program. This book could act as a refresher course, or it could be incorporated into your new employee orientation package. In support of your stated levels of conduct, this book will expand or reinforce your thoughts on service, appropriateness, interaction, and connecting.

Technicians/Staff. Wouldn't it be great for your career and esteem if every client you interacted with called your business and asked for you specifically? Maybe it occurs occasionally, but what if you could hone your people skills (your soft skills) and increase the number of clients who call and only want you to service their account? Your supervisor would take notice. I think it would put you on the fast track to better company exposure—promotion, increased salary, and/or more prestigious clients! Apply as many of these principles as you can, and you'll set yourself apart from your colleagues and/or your competition.

Anyone who manages or works inside a professional service business. This book isn't really written for the sandwich shop chains or the convenience store chains where customers are interchangeable. Although, it could help them as well. No, it's written for the professional service provider who desires to understand the criticality of repeat business, imperativeness of service, and, most assuredly, the importance of the client.

Believers in Relationships. Relationships branch out from every part of our lives. Some start through personal means, others business, while many are formed out of convenience, necessity, or other serendipitous methods. In all of these types of relationships, the parties involved must work together to make them succeed. Additionally, not everyone is proficient at relationships. For example, some people may be wonderful relationship partners personally but not in a business setting. Whatever your natural inclination toward relationships, this book can assist you in (1.) making your current ones stronger or (2.) helping you start new ones.

The ideas, principles, and philosophies in this book provide different ways service providers can connect to their clients in a genuine fashion. Doing it with the sole reason of generating sales is fake and transparent. The clients will figure that out and dump you. The connection has to be authentic, and your clients will appreciate it and respond in kind.

Part One: Core Principles

This section of Core Principles details the philosophies which allow the remainder of the book to work. Without fully integrating these ideas into your thoughts, lexicon, belief system, heart, and soul, you won't authentically adopt the methods illustrated herein. The only way to build or strengthen business relationships is through authentic, honest interactions. These Core Principles are meant to change your perspective on interacting with clients. They are the foundation of initiating your relationships, as well as maintaining them for a long time to come.

Core Principles: Your Mindset

It's Never Too Early

§

If you suck at your job, then no amount of polite behavior, niceness, or courtesy will save it.

The workplace is competitive. If you can't fix that computer or can't repair that A/C unit, then you're going to get fired by either your employer or your client. If you want to be the best plumber in your town, then study up. Learn. Excel. Become a humble authority. Build the best professional reputation you possibly can. Only at this point should you start to worry about the rest of the ideas and methods in this book.

THAT'S NOT TRUE.

When I was building my business, there were clients I gained because of the way I carried myself. I heard repeatedly I reminded clients of themselves when they were starting their own business. I was able to sell myself to clients—I could do what I said I could do, I would work hard for them, they'd be treated and billed fairly, and I was trustworthy. The truth was, when I was starting my business I had no idea how to run a business and I only had book smarts for my IT experience. That being said, how did I sell myself to those businesses?

I followed my own personal belief system of how I thought people should be treated. This belief system became the rules of conduct I imparted to my staff, as I hired and trained them. Now they are the basis for the philosophies in this book.

I treated my clients well, and they referred their friends and other business associates to me. Being a good student of my profession was a necessity; being nice was who I am; but being able to learn more skills while on the job was a blessing. It was an opportunity that came from demonstrating niceness, fairness, and honorable behavior. If I had been a jerk, those clients never would have hired me in the first place. They also wouldn't have allowed me to continue working for them, and they certainly wouldn't have referred me to their friends and/or to other businesses.

Therefore, it's never too early to incorporate these philosophies into your mind and behavior. Every positive interaction you have (no matter your skillset level) can lead to positive results for you personally and professionally.

Verbiage and Belief

§

Core Principles shouldn't be employed only at the verbal level, they must be changed mentally. Core Principles are beliefs. About you. About your profession. About your role. About your clients. Once the belief is changed inside of you, the rest becomes easier.

As a small or medium business owner, professional confidence is important, as is the professional display of that confidence. I recall when I started my business I was unsure of myself as a consultant, of the part I played in my client's lives, and in the marketplace. Then I learned multiple lessons about the parts I indeed played.

1. As a consultant, it wasn't my job to say "Yes" all the time. There were many times I said "Yes" when I should have said "No."

2. The part I played in people's lives became more and more important every day. Mentally, I became a protector of those families' livelihoods. If their business's critical data was lost, they could possibly go out of business, thus ruining how that family survived in the world. This made me take my professional responsibilities very seriously.

3. As for the marketplace, the one belief that made the most difference was this: I am a professional service provider; therefore, I don't have customers; I have clients. Grocery stores have customers because anyone can walk right in and buy something.

4. Professional service providers can pick and choose who

they work with; they have an expertise that others do not; they have a specific skillset the community cannot survive without.

5. Finally, professionals with clients are professionals with relationship skills. A customer comes into your life once and leaves. A gas station customer shops anywhere s/he wants, usually based on price and convenience. A client comes only to you because you've built a relationship with them. You are their resource for your field of expertise. Price and convenience become less important.

NOTE: By reading this book, you are attempting to better yourself, your company, and your client's existence. You desire to become a better professional. You want to set yourself, your company, and your list of services apart from your competition. These are the beginnings of the mental process you need to undertake in order to believe, without a doubt, that you are a professional service provider. Therefore, this book uses the word "client" rather than "customer." Professional service providers have clients. They don't have customers. By eliminating the word "customer," you are engaging your subconscious for assistance in this transformation.

Business Is Personal

§

It's business; it's not personal. WRONG! Your business *is* to make it personal. This book is about making it personal. Make it personal. When you relate personally with a client, you build a relationship. Relate is the root word of relationship. When a client (or any person for that matter) builds a relationship personally with you, then they will more often than not:

1. Call/Contact you again the next time there is a problem you can solve
2. Pay your bill on time
3. Tell their friends about you/your company
4. Maintain a long relationship/Find it hard to fire you

How do you initiate that type of relationship?

Be genuine. No matter what method you utilize to build a relationship, you must be genuine in your approach. Most people will sense inauthentic attempts. That will turn them off. It will make them think you're selling to them. People don't like to be sold to, and they don't need to be sold to. There are plenty of people/companies who offer the same services as you. Your potential clients can simply call another company, and they will, if they don't believe in your genuine authenticity.

Compliment something. Anything. When you enter someone's office for the first time, find something to compliment. A rug. The executive chair behind your client's desk. The desk. A decoration. The view out the window. The curtains or blinds. A painting or portrait on the wall. Empty space on the desk. You could say, "I would love to have empty space on my desk!"

These are all safe conversation starters. They will set the tone of the meeting/introduction as casual and comfortable. The client may tell you a story about the item you picked to compliment, which will bring about an emotion. Hopefully a good emotion; most of the time it will be. Plus, for you, it demonstrates you're attention to detail; it lets you take a moment to breathe and control your nerves, if you're nervous or scared; and, if you're very astute, you can pick up on the client's current mood, the way s/he communicates, and other personality traits.

Find a relatable object. If you compliment the client's desk, be prepared to back up the reason you complimented it. There better be a reason or a relatable story you can tell, if asked. If you compliment a picture of the client's children, then be ready for this question: "Do you have children?" You should have a relatable answer. For example, "Two. They look to be about the age of yours in that picture. 10 and 12." Or, "No, but I want four children. Everyone keeps telling me I'm crazy. Would you have had four? Or, am I indeed crazy?" If you compliment the desk, then say why you're complimenting the desk: "My father was an attorney and had a huge desk in his office. This desk reminds me of his."

Don't compliment, for example, the blinds in your client's office, if you don't know why you're complimenting the blinds. This will certainly show non-authentic compliments and will appear to be a sales tactic. You're not selling. Remember, you're making a new friend.

The reasons for your compliment should be personal, positive, and friendly. Don't supply a downer reason for complimenting the client's rug. "My friend died on a rug just like that one." Can you say "conversation staller?!"

Don't dwell on the compliment. The compliment is an icebreaker, not the reason for the conversation/meeting. Keep it short. Drop the compliment, allow the client to respond, and move on to the topic at hand—creating a lasting business relationship.

Keep private topics private. This is a professional setting after all. Don't share information that may be deemed inappropriate, too personal, or uncomfortable. Remember, those definitions are the client's to make, not yours to define. If what you say makes the client uncomfortable, then that makes everything after that a little harder. Discomfort creates an extra obstacle for you to surmount in your budding relationship. You can watch for body language cues, like your client sitting back in her chair, creating greater space between you and her/him. Another cue is when your client crosses her/his arms in front of her. This is a virtual shield between the two of you. You can research other body language cues on your own, but be mindful. If your client displays one of these cues, then you need to make changes in your conversation. Quickly.

Some other general ideas to keep in mind as you interact with your clients:

- Don't talk about an argument you had with your spouse.
- Don't talk about disciplining your children.
- Don't tell a sad story. Keep it positive.
- Don't talk about the usual off-limit/hot-button topics: politics, religion, and abortion. They're never comfortable conversations.
- Don't talk just about you. Stay focused on the client.

Vice versa, you can watch for positive body language, too, like:

- Posture – Keeping an open position. Arms crossed are a closed position. Hands at someone's side are an open position.
- Eye Contact – A person who is engaging in eye contact

throughout your conversations is listening to you and paying attention to you.

- <u>Smile</u> – Not a forced smile but a natural, warm smile.

Core Principles: Humanizing Your Clients' Experiences

BE HUMAN: The Panzer General Rule

§

What would you say if someone asked you why you care that your job gets done properly?

- I respect myself, so I do a good job at all I do.
- So I can get paid.
- So I don't get sued.
- It's my job to care.

All of these answers aren't part of building relationships.

Caring comes from somewhere else altogether.

It comes from the knowledge that somehow we are all connected. Perhaps we're connected through the common thread of being humans. The common experience, if you will. It might be something closer to home. Maybe you know the client through a friend. Perhaps your child goes to school with the client's child. Did you grow up in the same neighborhood? Maybe your dad knows his dad. Maybe a million different things.

The bottom line is this: you care because you should; because these are people who need your help; because we're civilized; because we would want someone to care about us if we ever needed help.

Think of an emergency room doctor. That doctor sees dozens (probably more than that) of people per day. The best ones care. S/He doesn't want you to die, to be in pain, or to be sick. S/He do what they can to help. S/He doesn't do a good job solely to collect a pay check, so s/he doesn't get sued, out of self-respect, or because it's her/his job to care. The ER doctor cares about the people they are serving. That's what you're doing in a professional service industry: providing a caring solution to a person's problem. Sometimes they show it by extending a simple touch or just listening to their patient.

You never know what other people are going through. You never know how important your fixing their problem is to them or what it means to them and their way of life.

A client, who passed away almost five years ago as of this writing, was a wonderful man. Intelligent. Handsome. Funny. And a schizophrenic. His computer was his a tool of enjoyment; one of few tools in which he found sanctuary from his own mind. A great fan of historical data, this man played a CD-based video game named Panzer General. He loved it. Talked about it every time I saw him. One time he played it for a few minutes to show me how it worked. It was delightful to see him smile at something when I'd seen him so many times agitated with his mental illness. I realized my keeping his computer in working condition allowed him happy times during his periods of lucidity.

When he passed away, his family asked me to clean up the computer for a relative to use. I found in the CD-ROM the Panzer General CD. With the families' permission, I kept the CD. I gently placed it in a clear CD case. I taped each side of the case to keep the CD protected inside it and stored it in my desk drawer. (*I still have it.*) Every time thereafter I opened my drawer, I was reminded that my job wasn't just to fix my clients' computers, servers, networks, etc., it was to care about my clients and my services were important to people.

Behind the break-fix nature of service industries, there is a need to correlate your job functions with a greater understanding of the possible human subtext. This results in a strong client/provider relationship. Personally, the result is knowing your job has meaning.

Through Their Eyes

§

One of the most important of the Core Principles deals with how you think. You have a busy day, need to get your paycheck deposited at the bank, have to pick up your kids from school, get them to soccer practice before going to Wednesday night church service. And you've been up since 5 AM! You're tired, have back-to-back appointments, and your personal life consists of being a bus driver. You're busy, to say the least. When you're this busy, it's easy to rush through your appointments; it's easy to finish the job completely and thoroughly but to forget about the client's experience.

For you to provide authentic service you must perform your provided service in the best, most professional, comprehensive, and honest way possible. However, the client's version of your service focuses on the authenticity of the experience.

For a client, having a service technician enter a home or office is an unnerving ordeal. No matter the service provider's industry (computer technician, lawyer, plumber, air conditioning repairman, etc.), the client is calling because something is wrong. Otherwise, there is little reason to have these service providers in their home or office, so the client is already on edge over the circumstances. They need a positive, authentic experience to walk away with. They need to be comforted, knowing you're in this with them.

Much like a restaurant's "atmosphere," the technician's appearance, attitude, cleanliness, task completion, and relationship building skills lend to the client's experience.

It is imperative to think of all you do from the perspective of the client because you don't win the client until the client wins a great experience from you. Even after a relationship has been built, you can lose a client because of a bad experience.

So, for your relationships to flourish, every interaction must be a positive, genuine, and authentic experience. To accomplish that, you must do whatever is necessary to authenticate the experience for your client.

Fight For Your Client

§

Every scenario is different. From the type of industry you work inside to the type of clients you have. There is no way to describe here what I mean by "Fight For Your Client" in a way that is applicable to those infinite scenarios, but this is close:

- You are the subject matter expert.
- So, in every situation that arises, you must advocate against all outside influences for the best results on your client's behalf.
- And you must do it honestly. Authentically.

What does that mean? When you advise your client, you can't have any agenda except your client's best interests. Yes, you need to sell your services and products, but you don't need to sell certain services and products to clients who don't need those services or products. I mean, you can … in the short term, but if you want a long-term relationship, then you can't. It won't take long before your clients figure out that you are providing them with solutions they don't need, and when they figure that out, the word-of-mouth that will be circulating won't be good.

After taking over the IT work at a new client's office, I found phones and Internet lines were being billed to the old IT service provider. After investigating, I discovered the previous IT service provider was a reseller of both the phone and Internet connections. Not only was the IT service provider collecting payment for services rendered, it was also making profit off the sale of those communication lines.

Further investigation revealed the IT provider's technicians were asked to consult on the best solution for the company in regard to phone and Internet lines. The technicians recommended the solution the provider resold. It wasn't the best solution for the client. It was the best solution for the provider and its profits.

I researched this for the client and found a solution with the same reliability, reputation, and scalability for half the price.

This client lost trust in their previous IT service provider, which was why they hired me, and this was a great illustration of why they distrusted him.

The provider was inauthentic in its consulting policies. It wasn't advocating *for* the client. The client figured it out and dumped the provider.

Core Principles: Virtue Adoption

Find Your Own Happiness

§

I don't know why, but in today's world happiness seems to be elusive. I talk to people every day who report being unhappy. Something is wrong in their life, and it's bringing them down in a huge way. Plus, they don't know how to change their lives. Maybe in this age of instant gratification we have lost the ability to think or plan for long-term happiness. Without constant stimulus, maybe we've lost the ability to be happy.

However, when you *are* happy, you want other people to be happy. Think about it. When you're single, what do all of your happily married friends try to do? Set you up on a date. They want you to be happy ... just like them!

To command you to be happy is unrealistic, at best. We all have stuff going on in our lives. I have stuff in mine I wish I didn't, but I do. I have to deal with it. However, it doesn't define who I am or how I am. You don't have control over the world, and you don't have control over someone else—your wife, your kids, friends, employees, clients, or strangers. You only have control over yourself and how you react.

Marriage troubles, kids' bad grades or bad behavior, and parent's health, for example, are hard to deal with, but you need to find a way to summon happiness around you during these times—for yourself and for your clients.

Running through each day in turmoil is stressful on your body, mind, and spirit. Your weight changes. If you have a medical condition, stress always seems to make it worse. You begin missing steps in your work because you're preoccupied. You forget tools and have to drive back to the office to pick them up. How can you be a good business owner, technician, worker, or friend when you're this stressed by turmoil?

Where do you find happiness? Search yourself. It's in there. Some people fish. Some shop. Join the gym. Exercise has been proven in study after study to make people feel better mentally and physically. Take walks. Go to a cooking class. Join a support group. Play tennis, basketball, or racquetball. Join an adult soccer league. The city where I live has an adult kickball league. I know dozens of people who play in it, and they all have a blast. Read a book.

Don't abuse alcohol. Don't overeat. Don't waste your time.

The techniques you use in hard times allows you to maintain your work focus. Maintaining your work focus allows you to serve your company and your clients better. Personally, it allows you to get through hard times.

One thing I've found helpful is studying whatever is wrong. If, for example, the problem is with my adolescent son's behavior, then I read a book about male behavior at the age of 13. It doesn't bring me happiness per se, but it does give me understanding of a boy at that age, which settles my brain and emotions, while it allows me to focus on my work and my own internal happiness. It converts the emotional thoughts into constructive ideas, thus limiting the mental cost of an unhappy situation. It doesn't solve the problem, but it aids in maintaining a professional concentration level.

True happiness, I believe, comes from inside. However, even true happiness has a hard time fighting against the negative events that occur throughout our respective lives. Search yourself. Get to know how you handle these negative situations. While you're happy, develop a plan based on what you know about yourself to deal with these situations, so you can maintain your focus on the tasks at hand, your professionalism, and your commitment to your clients. If you find a way to keep your mind not weighed down by personal drama, then your work and relationships will not suffer.

Patience Is More Than A Virtue

§

Patience is a gift. Some people have it, some don't. The ones who possess it have an advantage at building relationships. The people who don't possess it, should practice it.

What is so important about patience?

Here's the short answer: Patience leads to personal happiness … which leads to focus and diligence … which leads to better performance … which leads to higher client satisfaction … which leads to your superiors being excited to have you as a part of the team.

Patience leads to personal happiness. When you have patience, everyday troubles impact you less than if you don't have patience. Without it, every minor annoying incident immediately escalates emotionally and demands a reaction. This reaction is often the same explosion that goes off when a major annoying incident occurs. I can't imagine walking around every minute of my life on the edge of exploding reactions. That doesn't seem happy to me at all! The truth is, most annoying incidents aren't important enough to deserve an explosive reaction. I bet most of those incidents don't deserve a reaction at all. People occasionally make mistakes. The people I know who don't have patience for other peoples' trivial mistakes are narcissists who don't have the ability to put themselves in other people's shoes. They look at every situation as an inconvenience to themselves. They look at things only in regard to their experience, which means that everywhere these people go they are ready/expecting to explode in dissatisfaction over how things impact them. However, to have patience means you can witness an annoying incident and not let it bother you because you understand how the person could make an honest mistake. They *are* human!

Patience leads to better focus and diligence. There is no better time than when you're happy. All seems right with the world. Happiness breeds mental contentedness. When you're experiencing this happiness, your mental capacities can be laser-focused more easily than when you're not happy. When you're focused, you're more diligent. You do a better job while working on your assigned tasks. You double-check your work. You re-think your tasks to make sure you didn't miss a step or process. If you're studying a subject, then you retain the information better. You reread the chapter a second or third time until the information sticks. You don't get frustrated at yourself and ruin your concentration. If you're talking to a client and trying to explain a complicated concept, then you talk slower and more methodically. You answer the questions without getting annoyed. You patiently explain over and over the concept differently each time until the client understands to her/his desired level.

Patience leads to better performance. One time I wasn't focusing because a personal matter was weighing on my mind. I left my office and drove 47 miles to a client's office. When I parked my car in the client's office parking lot, I realized I'd forgotten to bring their computer with me, which was terrible since the only reason for my visit was to return the computer. I was so focused on the negative events occurring in my life that day I totally blew a chance to impress this client. Instead, I admitted my blunder to the client and drove back the 47 miles to my office, picked up the computer, and drove another 47 miles to their office. I put almost 100 extra, unnecessary miles on my car that day. Gas is expensive, and I wasted it. Plus, I had to reschedule the rest of my day. Total disruption! A little patience would have gone a long way — patience not to hurry out the door of my office; patience to take the time to pre-plan my appointment's necessary supplies.

Patience leads to higher client satisfaction. The client in the example above was gracious when I'd admitted my mistake, but they weren't satisfied. Once delivered and installed, the computer worked fine. The work I had done was solid. They paid their bill on time. However, they weren't impressed. After all, I made the appointment. Their staff made arrangements to be onsite at the time I selected. Since I forgot the computer, their staff sat for another hour and a half waiting for me to return. Their staff member had to rearrange his day because of me. The man still smiled at me when I left, and I still got a hand shake from him. But, he wasn't satisfied with the circumstances.

If I'd been more focused and diligent, then I would have remembered the computer when I left my office. I would have arrived at the client's office at the time I stated, the client would have received the computer quickly, and it would have worked perfectly. The client would have been satisfied.

Patience leads to your supervisors being excited to have you as part of the team. When you satisfy a client, sometimes s/he will call to compliment you and/or your work. That makes your supervisor very happy. Sometimes when you make a client happy, they ask for you by name the next time s/he calls with a new problem. That shows your supervisor that clients like you. When clients like you, they associate you with the company; therefore, they like the company. When supervisors are happy with their staff, they might pay commission, hand out raises, or promote them to supervisors themselves.

Patience is good to have for your co-workers too. Just like family, you can't pick your co-workers. Someone else picks them for you. That means there are many different personalities pushed into the same environment. This can be difficult. Patience allows you to deal with most people—even the most difficult. Another way to look at patience is that your co-workers see that virtue you have. They'll respect it. If they see you giving the office bad-apple patience, they'll respect that … and you. They'll know if you'll be patient with that guy, then you'll have patience for them as well. They'll know you're not judging them. That will attract them to you. You'll show yourself as a leader just because you're not reacting to the bad-apple.

Flexibility

§

Flexibility is a two way street—in one direction, you must have it; in the other direction, your client's must have it.

You. You are required to have flexibility. You absolutely have to. No way around it. There isn't a moment, in every professional service provider's career, that you don't need flexibility. Flexibility of time and schedule. Flexibility of knowledge. Flexibility of avenues of resolution. Every moment, step, conversation, phone call, email, text, or other new information changes every moment forever. You must be flexible enough to adapt with that change.

For example, as the technician when presented with problems (say a broken dishwasher), you've probably developed your own method of troubleshooting in order to resolve the problem. You go about determining the cause (probably) in the same way every time you have a broken dishwasher. Why? Because you know it works. However, what do you do when it doesn't work? When your method doesn't show the cause or doesn't resolve the problem? When you know you did it right, and the process should have fixed the machine?

I have known technicians who go through their process again and again, growing more and more frustrated with each pass through the troubleshooting steps. Once frustration sets in, a technician's thinking becomes clouded.

How do you handle this? Flexibility is the answer. You must be flexible enough with yourself to let go of your proven methods. You must be flexible enough to try new things, to take a step back from your usual ways of reasoning and consider the problem differently than you had been previously. If what you're doing doesn't work, try something else.

Clients. Clients typically don't start a relationship with flexibility, which is why you must train your clients to be flexible. Clients need to feel like they are your only client but realize you have others. There are two things at play here that go into your relationship with the client: feelings and realizing (knowing). The way you treat your client through premier service, dedication, loyalty, care, and understanding creates the "feelings" in this scenario. How you train them creates the "knowing."

In other chapters, I discussed telling your clients this:

"When I am with you, I don't answer my phone because I want you to have my undivided attention. After I complete my work with you, I call my voicemail and return phone calls. So, when you call and I don't answer, please leave me a voicemail because I am giving my undivided attention to another client."

Clients do understand this concept. They respect it because you're showing them value: "you have my undivided attention."

This is a form of training your clients. Training them to leave a message. Training them to be calm, to know you will take care of them as soon as possible. Training their expectations of you.

Furthermore, you can train your clients to be flexible as well. When a client calls, they believe their problem is the most important problem because it is impacting them and their workflow, blood pressure, frustration level, and who knows what else. Truth is, the problem they are reporting might not be your highest priority problem. The keys during this training period are fairness and communication. You have to demonstrate fairness in your process to them, other clients, and yourself. Tell them:

"If I have an appointment with you to install a new monitor, which is replacing your old but still-working monitor, and I get a call for a failed server, then I will have to call you to reschedule your monitor installation. A company of 25 people not being able to work off that server is more critical than your new monitor replacement. However, when the situation is reversed and your server fails, I will reschedule my other clients because your server is more critical than their issues at that moment. It's a give and take relationship."

In the past, I have told clients this during sales meetings in regard to response time. It addresses the issue openly, trains them from the start, and sets the expectation that when they have an emergency (a genuine emergency), they will be a priority. I've never had a client not accept that answer.

That philosophy and training worked throughout my IT consulting career.

Companies that have "customers" do not use flexibility. Take the cable company, for example. Stereotype, yes, but appropriately so. They give you a four hour window and you better be there when they show up. If not, it could be days before you get another appointment. If you are reading this book, then you don't want to have customers. You want clients. Clients need flexibility.

You can develop your own industry-specific flexibility standards and start training your clients today. Be sure you describe in your mantras how the client will get their value from you. If you detail that to them, they'll be flexible for you.

Notes

§

Before delving into the next ideas, methods, philosophies, principles, and best practices, examine again each of the Core Principles again. Write down any ideas of your own in relation to the ideas presented here. How do they apply to your job? To your client interactions? Do you agree or disagree with the principles presented? Use this examination as a conversation started, either with your staff or your manager or your business's owner.

_____

_____

_____

_____

_____

_____

_____

_____

_____

_____

_____

Part Two: Appearance

It's not a coincidence I start the post-core sections of this book with the topic of Appearance. It's often how we are first judged by people we meet. Or, should I say, how we are judged by people *before* we meet? "First impressions are lasting impressions." As a visual species, we tend to judge first impressions on people's appearances, which begs these questions in relation to building relationships:

- What judgment do you want to impress upon your business colleagues by your appearance?
- Are you representing physically in your appearance what you want people to think of you?
- Is your presentation consistent within your professional circle?

Without stifling your individuality, the way you exhibit yourself is vital to your relationship success and must be displayed appropriately based on your level and field of profession. Use this section to assist you in your physical presentations to your business colleagues.

Appearance: Carrying Yourself

Confidence

§

Confidence is an ever-elusive thing for some people, even mythological. What it is for one person, it isn't for another. What works to demonstrate confidence for one person, doesn't work for another. What makes one person when acting confident look obnoxious makes another person seem charismatic? It's ridiculous and hard to define.

Yet, you have to have it in spades.

If you research confidence, you'll find words like cool, swagger, attitude, and even je ne sais quoi. But, again, if you fake it, you'll appear foolish. In your business relationships, people think the nicest cars show success, and success equals confidence. That's not true. Rich people aren't necessarily the most confident people. FYI ... many people who are driven to succeed are simply working to fill a hole inside them dug by insecurity and self-esteem issues; they think being successful will make them worthwhile. So put that notion aside. Anyone can have confidence, and any person may not have it.

Confidence is:

- Being self-assured
- Feeling secure
- Acting respectful to yourself and others
- Maintaining strict honesty and ethics
- Working Hard
- Being funny
- Staying positive
- Being non-judgmental
- Remaining composed in all situations

Confidence is not:

- Being patronizing
- Being cocky
- Acting superior to other people
- Displaying rudeness
- Being Insensitive
- Bragging
- Boasting

So, how do you show confidence? How do you have confidence?

Continue bettering yourself. This shows you care about yourself and your future, as well as showing you are confident in your abilities to grow personally and professionally.

Always try to do the right thing. This will help you sleep at night. The purest, genuine, and authentic confidence results from making good choices personally and professionally. Plus, you won't be tired.

Like yourself. You're awesome. You know it. Let others see that you know it. Do something you like to do. This will grow your confidence without any extra effort. When you do something you enjoy, you feel better. All around. It'll show.

Be yourself. If you're bettering yourself, trying to always do the right thing, and you like yourself, then being yourself will be easy. You'll have something to talk about, and you'll do it confidently.

Listen to people. You know what you think about things. Why don't you engage the other person to find out what they think about those same things? Expand your frame of reference by exposing yourself to different opinions than the ones you have. If asked directly a question, answer it with all your charisma, but then turn it back to the other person. The more you listen, the more you'll learn about that person, the business, the company history, and the clientele.

Still unsure how to be confident? Look at it this way. Think of what you are most confident about. Is it your work? Is it sports? Is it fashion? What is it? Video yourself talking to a friend about that one thing. Talk long enough with your friend that you forget the camera is recording. Eventually, stop the recording and watch it. Watch it and look at the way you're communicating, the words you're using, and the posture of your stance.

Do you ever reach out and touch your friend? Is that a positive touch? Affirming touch? Sympathetic touch. What prompted you to reach out and touch her/him?

Are you looking your friend in the eye? Or, are you avoiding eye contact. If you see yourself avoiding eye contact, then review the tape. Were you uncomfortable about something going on at the time of the avoidance? Did your friend say something you didn't like? Were you talking about something you were unsure of? Why did you look away?

Were your arms crossed? Were your hands in your pockets? Or, were you using your hands to talk?

Here's a clue to how you're doing. Make sure you both have a drink in the video. A glass of water is fine. If you're exuding the most confidence in the conversation with your friend, then watch closely. When you get a drink, your friend will too. However, if your friend gets a drink and then you do, then your friend is exuding more confidence. That means you have more practicing to do.

Continue studying yourself. Search your weaknesses and strengths. Study other people and other conversations. You'll pick up on confident gestures, postures, and other confident movements. Apply them to yourself, as needed. Find what works for you. Doing this will show you care about bettering yourself.

Surround yourself with confident people. If you want to be confident, then involve yourself with confident people. You can watch how they behave up close. You can get a front-row seat to confidence. Plus, it will rub off on you. Same thing as success. If you want to be successful, surround yourself with successful people. You'll learn how to be successful, how to act successful, and how to dress successful. Act, dress, and be now who you want to be in the future.

Get a life coach. Life coaches listen to you. They're on your side. They offer differing viewpoints on your life's various circumstances. They help you see through life's fog to find its sunlight. They are motivating. It's never a bad idea to have that kind of person in your life. If your friends are not able to direct you in the way you need, hire a life coach. If you don't want to share your needs with your friends, hire a life coach. Whatever your goal, they can help, and we all need as much of that as we can obtain.

The key is this: Know who your best person is and do whatever it takes to be that person.

Appearance: Presentation Is Everything

Not-Too Casual Friday

§

I'm all for casual Fridays. There's something refreshing going into the weekend in a comfortable pair of pants. However, I have seen casual Friday disasters! Skirts too short. Jeans too tight. Shorts. Flip flops. Not good.

If your office allows casual Friday, it's a privilege. Don't abuse it. You don't want to lose the privilege.

Use your typical dress policy to determine proper casual Friday attire. If your office is a suit-and-tie office Monday through Thursday, then don't show up in shorts on Friday. Wear khakis and a button up long- or short-sleeve shirt. For ladies, if you normally wear a business suit, then wear a tasteful, knee-length skirt or a casual business pants suit and a blouse that expresses your personality. If your office has a business casual daily policy, then jeans may be acceptable on Friday. **Note:** Not jeans that are stylishly tattered and torn or skin-tight.

Base what you wear on what clients you'll see that day. No matter the day of the week, if you're interacting with clients face-to-face, be professionally presentable. Don't wear flip flops. Don't show up unshaven. Wear something befitting of the professional you are.

I went into a client's office one time and found the receptionist wearing a football jersey. Granted it was Friday and the weekend before a big game, but the jersey was very large. It looked like all she was wearing was the jersey and flip flops. This was a very prominent lawyer's office. I don't know if the receptionist knew no clients were coming in for appointments, but I went in to the office. I saw it. And now I'm putting it into a book, so ... you never know who you'll see when you go to work.

Present yourself professionally. Even on casual Friday.

Slob

§

It was a national holiday. My office was closed, but I received an emergency call from a new client. She couldn't reach her IT vendor. Her server was booting in a loop. Over and over, it was restarting without loading all the way to the login screen. She, a dentist, was thinking of canceling all of her appointments the following day because there was no way to use her X-ray machine, Quickbooks, and dental software without the server being fully functional. She said of her IT consultant, "I always wondered about him. He was recommended to me, but he was so sloppy. Pants. Hair. Shirts." She shook her head. "Sloppy."

At the time, I was wearing a nice T-shirt, khakis, and casual shoes. I hadn't shaved yet. It was a holiday after all, and I was being pulled away from family. She knew she was imposing on my holiday and the server was having a REAL problem, so I knew she wouldn't care what I was wearing. The urgency in this case outweighed all other circumstances. I rushed over to her office without changing my attire. When she described her sloppy IT guy, I laughed, pointing to my appearance, and said, "That must be what you think of me, too."

"Oh, no," she replied. "You're fine. You're clean. Personable. Know what you're doing. Very professional."

I had only been onsite for about 20 minutes. She didn't really know if I knew what I was doing. She didn't know how professional I really was. As bad/casual as I thought I was, she thought I was more put together than the guy she'd been paying for two years.

I'm certainly no fashion icon, but I try very hard to represent myself professionally, even when I'm dressed down. Most of the time, representing yourself in a professional manner starts with your choice of attire. If you package yourself in dress pants and a button-up shirt, you act differently and feel differently about yourself than when you wear jeans and a T-shirt. It's true. Additionally, people judge you differently. Right or wrong, they do.

Therefore, figure out how to represent yourself professionally.

If you're an owner of a business, get your staff uniforms, depending on your industry. Or, set specific office attire policies.

If you're a technician or staff member, set yourself apart by dressing well. You'll feel better, your boss will think more positively about you, and your clients will be impressed.

Match your shoes and your belt.

Match your socks to your pants or shirt.

When your shirts or pants are tattered or have holes, get rid of them.

Don't wear torn shoes.

If your shirt should be tucked in, keep it tucked in all the time.

If your shirt isn't one that's tucked in, make sure it covers the old plumbers-crack, beer belly, or belly ring.

Wear clothes that fit—nothing too tight *(please!)* and nothing too loose.

Purchase a fashion magazine to get ideas, ask friends, or review online dressing guides.

You could be the best technician or business owner in the whole world, but if you don't represent yourself professionally, people will find it harder to believe in you because it will look like you don't believe in yourself. If you don't care about yourself enough to present yourself professionally, then how can they believe you will care about their problems professionally?

Don't Be Gross

§

There's no delicate way to get into this topic, so I'm just going to throw it out there. I can't imagine anyone will disagree or will need extra explanation, so it's best to just get right to it.

Wear proven deodorant.

Keep your teeth brushed.

Check your nose for ... *(I'm just going to say it)* boogers ... before you meet with a client.

Keep your ears clean of wax and debris.

Keep mints handy for good breath.

Keep your fingernails clean.

Don't chew your fingernails to a nub.

Keep your hands washed.

Check the corners of your mouth for white spittle.

Verify you don't have any food in your teeth. No bread, pepper, or lettuce, etc.

Check your eye corners for crust.

Solve the dandruff problem, if you have one.

Bring a handkerchief, if you sweat a lot. Wipe when needed.

For men, prior to entering your first stop after shaving in the morning, make sure you don't have any dried blood on your face, chin, or neck. Ladies, check your legs for the same.

If you wear glasses, keep them clean of gunk and other build-up.

In summary, show you have respect for yourself. Don't let your client walk away thinking of you as the guy with bad breath.

Appearance: Grooming

The No-Personality Face

§

My 13 year old son laughs when I tell him my face is my money maker, but it's true on some level. I'm no model (*which is why he laughs when I say that*), but a clean, well-maintained face is a professional necessity. You can go into any business situation with a conservative face.

So, what's a conservative face for men and women? A lot of things. It's easier to focus on what isn't a conservative face.

For both men and women, try to avoid neck and face tattoos. I've seen women with very small tattoos behind one of their ears or on the back of their necks. This is fine as long as in business environments your hair can hide it.

For women, don't wear too much makeup. We've all seen this women—the one who uses a spackling knife to put on her makeup. It's clownish, and it makes people wonder what she's hiding under that layer of makeup. When people notice that about a woman, then they aren't thinking about what that woman is bringing to the table for business purposes.

For men, keep your face clean-shaven; your hair groomed; your eye brows trimmed; and your nose hairs tidy. Same thing with your ear hair. *(Actually, all that goes for women, too.)* If you prefer a beard, then keep it manicured. Don't *(I have seen this and is one of my reasons for writing this section)* draw designs in your beard. Don't! *(For that matter, don't do it in your hair anywhere on your body!)* In fact, keep your facial hair style simple. No mutton chops. No A la Souvarov. No Fu Manchu.

No Dali. No handlebar and chin puff. No Balbo. No Winnfield. No Klingon. No Hulihee. No Franz Joseph. No Napoleon III Imperial. No Super Mario.

As in all these chapters, each business industry and business owner has their own definitions of appropriateness. These are general ideas. What's inappropriate in one business environment is acceptable in another. The point is:

- What you don't want is to draw attention to your face in a negative light, so don't do anything that would cause someone to look at your face and think, "What is that about?"
- You want them to look at you and think, "This will be a good business transaction. My first impression is sight, and I am impressed at her/her professionalism."

Appearance: Vehicle As Show

You Are Your Car; Your Car Is You

§

I've driven a 25 year old Buick Le Sabre. I've driven a Ford Mustang. A Chevy Malibu. A Saturn. A Nissan Xterra. A Mitsubishi Galant. A BMW and a Mercedes. It didn't matter which of these cars I was driving, the car's appearance said something about me. One or more of these cars were littered with fast food wrappers, empty and used coffee cups, mail, newspapers, soda cans, clothes, shoes, sports equipment, and who knows what else at this point. And some of these cars were kept immaculate.

The dirty car stated that I didn't care about my surroundings. I bet someone could argue that I wasn't happy during that period of life. Perhaps I felt lost, unmotivated, and without direction. Maybe even lazy. That may have been true. But, when I went on a date, I'd clean that dirty car and make it look like new. So, even then I knew something was wrong with the way I kept my car. I knew a clean car impressed.

As a business professional, you never know when you'll be in someone else's vehicle, and you never know when someone will be in yours. Keep it clean. It doesn't have to be perfect, but keep it presentable. When your car is clean and presentable, you also appear clean and presentable. You appear to care about your possessions, your role in life, how you see yourself, and how others will view you.

People make snap judgments. You can wear a pristine, perfectly fitted suit, but inviting your client into a car filled with garbage, clothes, and other debris will only result in a negative judgment of you, your business acumen, your product, and ultimately of how you will care for your client.

It's not about the car you drive. It's about how you present yourself. How you present your car. You are your car. Your car is you. It's an extension of how put together you are. Or are not.

How does this apply to your interactions with your clients? How does this apply to your clients knowing you care for them and will create a human bond? How does this apply to you going the extra mile to resolve your client's problems? There are more communication types than just words. In addition to words, communication is a combination of actions, images, perceptions, thoughts, and emotions. Depending on the sender or the receiver of the communication, the result of that communication is positive or negative. By creating an environment most likely to result in a positive perception, you create nonverbal communication to the client that you will care for them. Caring for your car is positive, unspoken communication. Caring for your own appearance is positive, unspoken communication. The same as wearing a nice suit is positive, unspoken communication. The same as smiling. It's all good. The clients who see this will almost definitely see you in a positive light, thus resulting in believing you will take care of them and their needs.

Notes

§

Before delving into the next ideas, methods, philosophies, principles, and best practices, examine again each of the Core Principles again. Write down any ideas of your own in relation to the ideas presented here. How do they apply to your job? To your client interactions? Do you agree or disagree with the principles presented? Use this examination as a conversation started, either with your staff or your manager or your business's owner.

_____

_____

_____

_____

_____

_____

_____

_____

_____

_____

Part Three: Work

If your client perceives a positive impression of you from your physical appearance and provides you the opportunity to perform your professional service, then you have passed the first impression test. You have been granted the ability to (1.) prove your client's impression correct (that you're a fine, upstanding member of society who can be looked upon as a professional resource) or (2.) prove your client's impression wrong (that, despite how professional you appear, you are not very good at your job).

To succeed in creating relationships with your clients, you must perform the functions of your duties comprehensively, authoritatively, and with your client's best interest at the heart of your every task. This section (and book) cannot cover every aspect of every industry's job duties. It does attempt to point out very specific steps you can take in order to create the highest percentage of successful opportunities to facilitate the initiation, building, and maintenance of client relationships. Implement the following work practices and ideas into your overall perspective, and they will help you earn and keep client relationships.

Work: Performance Best Practices

Under Promise

§

Under promise and over deliver. A client once said that to me when I told him I'd return his computer to him the next day. He knew the problem with the computer would take longer to fix than one day, but I was over-confident in my abilities, or under-informed as to the extent of the problem. Perhaps he was letting me off the hook, or, more likely, since he was a business consultant, he was teaching me a lesson. One now that I am passing on to other people.

Relationships are built on trust. The inherent trust between the technician/company and the client is important. The client trusts that you will provide excellent service while delivering a product and the technician/company trusts that the client will pay for the service/product. Broken promises destroy that trust and possibly that relationship.

Never promise what you can't deliver. If you don't know how to do something that your client needs, don't say you can do it. What good does that do? You'll end up with a task that's outside of your expertise. What happens if you fail at that task? Your relationship is harmed. Additionally, you add undue stress to your, probably, already too-full plate.

Similarly, if you're asked a question that you don't know the answer to, then don't answer it like you're an authority on it. There is nothing wrong with saying you don't know. I prefer this response, "Off the top of my head, I'm not sure. I can find out and get back to you." Why give an answer when the client could find out the truth from another source? Then you become less of an authority figure to your client because s/he now knows you gave them a bogus reply. That's never good. How can they trust your next answer to be true?

Communication is the key to your relationships. In my example from the opening paragraph of this philosophy, I told a client I'd have his computer back to him the following day. Let's say he didn't let me off the hook and was expecting it the next day. What are my choices when the end of the next day comes and the project isn't complete? I can keep working on it and deliver it the following day, one day late. In this case, the client wonders all night long where his computer is, if the problem was harder than everyone thought, how much more is this costing him, and when will he actually get the computer back. No, that won't work. If you're constantly thinking about your interactions with a client as that client's "experience," then why put your client through those thought processes, through that negative experience?

At the very moment I know I won't get the computer back to him, I have to communicate that to the client, either in person or via a phone call. You explain the complications: the problem is harder than originally anticipated; the problem isn't harder, but the resolution is just taking more time than expected; emergencies arose with other clients; or scheduling conflicts caused a re-working of the calendar. Most of the time, unless the client is completely stressed about the situation, the communication is all the client needs.

Clients just want to know what's going on with their work, how the work is progressing, and when the problem can be resolved and normalcy returned. If it takes a week rather than a day, then it takes a week. Just keep them posted every step of the way.

The best policy is to contact your client with a progress report before s/he contacts you asking for one.

Thanks. When the job is finally completed and the client is happy, make sure you thank your client for her/his patience, as you worked diligently to resolve their problem/finish their work. You can do it in person, through a handwritten note, or through a small reduction of fees. Any way you can show the client you appreciate their continued trust in you would be a good thing to do. They'll remember it. I have done that numerous times, because I often over-promised. In response, I'd oftentimes receive a hand written note with the payment in the mail, saying "Thanks for your note" or "Thanks for the rebate".

Change your timeframe. The "Thank you" from me was an apology for the over-promise. Their reply was an acceptance of that apology and an appreciation for keeping them updated on the progress throughout the course of the project. That's great, but you don't want that to keep happening. You should really be working on not over-promising. If your typical reply is that you can turn around the project in one day, then change that to three days. It allows you time in case other emergencies come up. Don't wait, though, until the day before to do the work. Start on it immediately. Because here's the moral of the lesson: if you promise three days and return it in one day, then you've exceeded your client's expectations. That's when you get referrals from your clients to new clients. That's when the relationship really starts to pay dividends.

Don't Take Shortcuts

§

Your work is your product, and it defines you. That's the truth in our society. The quality of work you do, good or bad, is how people will see you. It's how people will describe you to other people. You're in control of that.

For example, don't finish your task, finding out there are two screws left over, and leave it like that. Those two screws are needed somewhere in that device. They're probably pretty important. Maybe they keep a cooling fan stabilized inside the machine. Without those screws, the fan could loosen and cause a terrible vibration. Maybe the fan won't work at all now without the screws, creating too much heat inside the machine, which results in the machine breaking down. Instead of that, take the machine apart and find where the remaining two screws belong. Do your job and do it right.

There's an example that can be made for every business, as well as almost every situation—personal or professional. Plumbers, attorneys, realtors, coaches. Every profession, every relationship. I, of course, can't go into all of them, but I want you to focus on the main ideas that follow.

Don't knowingly shortcut your job functions. This can be considered stealing. Say that you're paid by the service. If you don't complete the full service checklist, then you're stealing. The client is paying for something they didn't get. They paid the full price but didn't get the full service. This is deceptive. Plus, doing so can cause serious repercussions. Think of an airline mechanic. What if he takes shortcuts? Or a surgeon? We've all heard stories about sponges being left inside people. How about a roofer? He takes a shortcut and your roof leaks causing extensive damage.

What will *your* shortcut cost people during surgery? Or yourself? Or your company? Stealing, damage, death, or lawsuits. Save everyone (including yourself) trouble and just do your job the right way.

Do your job and do it right (fully and completely), and double-check your work. Show the pride you have for yourself. Show your level of self-respect. Any proud, self-respecting worker wants to do her/his best in their every task. When you do your best, you're showing your pride and self-respect. People will appreciate that, see it, and view you in a respectable fashion. That means they'll call you again! They'll be happy to pay you a second, third, and fourth time.

Not doing your job right is not caring about your client. And you must care about your clients. For small businesses, in particular, clients return because of your quality work *AND* your care for them. The quality work they receive is *what* they get from you. Your care is *why* they call you. Any company's staff can do quality work. But few company staffers care about their clients. I'm not saying you have to "love" your clients. I'm saying you have to care about them. You have to humanize your clients. They are why you have a business after all.

Let's revisit the roofer who takes a shortcut. The roof leaks. Water pools in the attic and finds its way into a wall. Not enough water that the home owner notices, but just enough to cause mold to grow. How does the roofer know that the homeowner's daughter is sickly and the presence of mold will make her sicker? He doesn't. But, if he had humanized his clients, he'd understand there could be consequences to him taking shortcuts. There are potential consequences to every choice we make. The roofer has to care about his clients in such a way that he forces himself to do the job right. This is a different motivation than not getting paid or getting sued.

You have to care about your clients.

Respect Your Surroundings

§

When you are in your client's office or home, you are their guest. As such, you should treat their office and/or home with respect, and it doesn't matter in what condition the office or home exists. You are not allowed to leave your garbage behind, if you are in an office that is inhabited by a hoarder or if you are in a palatial home with three maids. There is no excuse ever for leaving your trash behind.

Follow these simple rules to demonstrate that you respect the client's space, even if the client doesn't respect it.

Entering a home. When your client opens her front door, wait for her to invite you inside. If she doesn't, then ask, "May I come in." I know; it sounds weird. Why else would you be there, except to go inside and work? By the client's invitation or you asking to enter, you set up a relationship with the client in which the client is in charge. That's important because she is indeed in charge. This is no different than being in the reception area of a business and awaiting the receptionist's permission to proceed beyond her desk.

Wipe your feet. After you're invited or granted access to the home, wipe your feet on the front door mat. This shows care and respect for the interior of the home or building. Do the same thing before entering a business.

Trash removal. Whatever boxes, containers, bags, or other packaging you bring into the office/home with you, take away with you. The only exception is if the client offers to throw away the trash for you, in which case you protest and try genuinely to take the trash with you.

This shows your commitment to servicing and not imposing on your client. However, if they vehemently insist, it's all right to leave it in their hands. Sometimes refusing to give in to their insistence is ruder than leaving the garbage behind. You'll have to know the difference.

Vacuum. If your work includes anything that may have caused dust or small debris to land on the floor, then clean it up as best as you can. Use a broom and dust pan or a vacuum. If your work commonly causes this problem, then you should carry one or both with you at all times. If not, then ask to borrow a broom or a vacuum. Whatever you do, do not leave with that floor being dirty. At least, find a paper towel, dampen it, and use it to collect the dust.

Double-check. My work would often require me to open packages, whose content was organized with ties. When this happened, I put those ties, as I untied them, into my pockets, so they wouldn't accidentally drop onto the carpet where a vacuum might pick it up and be damaged. I also didn't want to inadvertently leave them on the client's desk or counter. If left on the desk, I imagined the client would surely see it and find it annoying to have to pick up after me. If that were to happen, then the client would see a crack in the line of service provided. Double-check your area. Do whatever you need to do in order to leave the area in which you worked the same (if not better) than when you arrived.

The overall point of these tasks is to set you apart from all the other service professionals in the world. Go the extra mile. We all say we do, but most of us typically don't. You can, and you'll be rewarded for it. Clients who know you take care of them appreciate you and return that care. What goes around comes around.

Work: Process Best Practices

Organize Everything

§

Arriving at a client's office or house with a notebook is a great idea. Notebooks are good for keeping your time recorded, documenting the work you performed, and writing yourself notes on points of follow-up with the client. I carry one with me most of the time.

However, it's not a good idea to arrive with a disorganized notebook. There's something terribly unprofessional about standing in the lobby of your client's office only to have your disorganized notebook open up and throw dozens of papers all over the floor. **Never greet your client when you're on all fours!** Picture it! You're chasing papers all over the lobby, the receptionist is watching you, laughing or rolling her eyes. Someone else is waiting for their appointment. One or both of them will offer to help you pick up your papers. Then the person you're meeting enters the lobby and finds you and the two other people on the floor chasing your papers.

Terrible!

And don't forget to bring a pen. Nothing worse than having the above example occur and then have to borrow a pen from the client.

Keep your car organized. As mentioned in another principle, the care you give your car can illustrate the care you'll give your client. You never know when you will need to give someone a ride. Keep it clean and organized. Know where things are that you'll need in your car. A screwdriver. A notepad. Lip balm. Lotion. Your license and registration. Your spare tire. Know how to open your trunk and your hood, to turn on your hazard and interior lights, and to utilize your Cruise

Control.

Keep your office and desk clutter-free. I was 100% guilty of this offense. I told people my office was a working office not a show office. It seemed the papers kept stacking up, the mail was dropped everywhere, and old computer parts were strewn about. I organized my office a thousand times. Each time, within a few months, it was overpowered by clutter. I was so busy working that I didn't have time to organize my office. It was embarrassing when people came inside.

Files must be maintained. Keeping accurate filing systems, either electronically or physically, is a must. No sense in keeping information, if you're going to have to spend hours finding it. Every business owner fears the IRS. What if you get audited? How much time away from making money would you have to spend organizing the information they would request of you? File by category alphabetically. That's easy to figure out. Plan it out before implementing.

Keep your brain functioning optimally. Stay active. Good blood flow through your brain keeps your brain working right. Exercise! Eat right! Quality vitamins and nutrients keep the brain functioning well. Don't over-indulge in alcohol. I love a good, strong beer, but too much leaves me hazy the next day. I try not to drink at all during the work week, or if I do, then I limit it to a couple of glasses of wine spread throughout the week. Certainly don't drink every night. Plus, doing all of this will help you maintain a good weight, which also helps your brain and energy levels stay high. There is something awesome about having a client call you with a question and you immediately can recall their layout and answer the question right off the top of your head. Bam! Here's your answer.

Awesome! You're the best! Thanks!

Document Everything You Do

§

Few rules I employed when I started my business lasted throughout the life of the company. This, however, was one that did last the whole time. It takes time, yes, but the payoff is great! It helps different aspects of your workplace.

It helps the client. When I would document the problem a client experienced and the work performed to resolve the issue, the client was very impressed with the attention to detail. They didn't necessarily understand the technical aspects of what was written/typed on the invoice, but they could tell I did a ton of work to fix their problem! Clients don't want to be handed a $300 invoice with a one line description of the work performed.

It helps your credibility. When a client sees that much detail put into an invoice, they know you've taken the time to really care about solving their problem. Additionally, it adds to the honesty and trust factors associated with your clients. You are showing them every step you performed. It shows your clients you have nothing to hide. They like that!

It helps you in the future. I had clients call me a year after I changed their passwords on their wireless routers and ask me for the password. I checked my documentation and found it. Sent it within a couple minutes. It saved me from going back to the house or business to access the router and find it for them. Moreover, it also saved them the cost of me going to their house or place of business again. Because I kept documentation, I was able to provide the information quickly and without any additional cost to the client. The result of that is the client understands I wasn't nickel-and-diming them.

It helps co-workers. If someone on your team goes home sick or gets fired and you have to follow-up with one of their clients, wouldn't it be great to pick up right where he left off, performing none of the same tasks twice? You could just read the notes and head into the client's office or home ready to go. Saves time. Saves the client money. Most importantly, it lends a perception of credibility and professionalism to both the technician and the company.

It hurts your competition. One of my clients employed a remote worker a thousand miles away. That worker hired a local company to come in and set up his computer system. The client's accounting representative contacted me to ask me about the other IT company's invoice. Her complaint was that the invoice was for $575 worth of labor. The detail on the invoice read: "Setup computer and printer." This client was used to my documentation style (see below). She was angry at the other company for not detailing their costs.

So how should you document?

1. Write things down as you go, so you don't have to remember later. I had a ticketing system, which allowed me to update the tickets from the client's computer. I'd connect to my online ticketing system and just enter whatever data was necessary to resolving the problem. If I didn't have access to the system, I used my iPad to enter it into my ticketing system or I wrote it down in a notebook and typed it up later.

2. Be specific. Record what the client reported, then what you found the problem to be, and finally all the steps you took to resolve the problem.

3. List any inventory it took to repair the problem.

4. Show your time.

5.   Show the cost of everything.

Talk to your manager about the best style to use for this documentation, and you'll get a nice pat on the back for your initiative. If you're the manager, decide on the style and push the style down to your staff through training. Any style will work as long as it's uniform across all of your staff.

Write Well

§

Not everyone writes well, and I'd bet some of the clients won't even know if you're writing properly or not; however, the ones that know proper writing will see it … and they'll remember you for it. If your workplace decides documentation is the way to go, then follow these few steps to make sure you don't lose credibility with the client.

1. Make sure your words are spelled right. If you're unsure of a word's spelling, then don't use that word. Or, using your smartphone, look it up online. Whatever you do, don't leave a misspelled word on the invoice.

2. Don't use slang words, like in this sentence: "Waxed the beemer." That doesn't work. Instead write, "Technician waxed the blue 2012 BMW 328i."

3. Provide details. Explain what you did. What type of wax did you use? Did you buff the car? What color was the car? Did you clean the wheels? Is that a service fee or an hourly fee?

4. Spell the client's name correctly. It's perfectly acceptable to ask for the correct spelling. Spelling it wrong is disrespectful.

5. Not everyone was an English major in college. It's fine if you don't know what a dangling participle is. The point is to keep it simple. If writing isn't your strong suit, then remember that simple and correct is better than complex and wrong.

Work: Conflict Avoidance and Resolution

Be Fair and Responsible

§

While I know relationships (even client-technician relationships) can end with a sense of bitterness, it seemed all the companies that hired me in order to get away from their old IT company didn't like or trust the IT company. Some of the reasons I heard: one tech was an alcoholic; one company over-charged; another one charged for phone calls; another never called the client back; more than one never came on site; some only showed up to collect a check; and one technician took money for a new server, cashed the check, and never showed up with the server.

I didn't want that to be me.

I didn't want to be described liked that.

I've enjoyed being nice to people. It's something that comes naturally to me, and it makes me feel good when I can do it. Part of that is why I enjoyed my work so much. I suppose I have a people-pleaser personality. My hourly rate was reasonable. It wasn't the least expensive, but it wasn't astronomically high either. My billing practices were fair. They were explainable and justified.

That, to me, was the equivalent to being fair and reasonable.

People genuinely seemed happy to pay me and call me again when they needed assistance. I was good at my work. I didn't hide things from the client and documented my processes and resolutions. I listened, cared, and worked with compassion. I found my own personal happiness in helping my clients, and I didn't tell their secrets.

I don't hang my head when I see past customers. I believe I

treated my clients in a fair and reasonable fashion, so I have no reason to hang my head. I operated ethically. I treated my clients with the same level of respect and honor.

I am privileged to have relationships with many business people and am delighted to have them as friends. I often hear people say how much they respect one of those men or women. I want to be like them. I was recently at lunch with one of these men. He left before me. When I was on my way out the restaurant door, a gentleman stopped eating and flagged me down. He said, "You are keeping good company. That man is wonderful. A good man." I smiled and told him I felt the same way.

That's what I want people to say about me!

Wouldn't it be nice for them to be saying that about you?

Take control of your actions and attitudes. Be fair and reasonable in all your interactions. It will gain you return business, respect, and admiration. Not only that, people will see you as a model. They'll want to be just like you.

Limit Conflicts

§

The downside to being fair and reasonable is that some people will try to take advantage of you. *YOU CANNOT LET THEM.* Being fair and reasonable is a strength. No one should see it as a weakness. You must combat this image.

Many small businesses work on credit. That means you provide a service, bill the client, and then the client pays. In these relationships, you (your business) are the one exposed to loss. And many times (most times) the fees you charge are too low to hire an attorney to collect, if they go unpaid. So, how do you combat that exposure?

What follows is a list of conflict-avoiding processes and conducts for you to employ with your clients.

Use a service agreement. These agreements outline the relationship you expect to have with the client, how you'll be paid, and what work you'll perform. This grants both parties knowledge of expectations. You and the client can refer to this document to clear up disagreements. It's a good tool, but you have to keep up your end of the expectations. If you don't, then this document will haunt you. But, if you're following the ideas in this book, then you'll exceed the parameters defined in this document. Thus, limiting exposure to conflict.

Discuss your fees. Make sure the client knows how much you charge. Or, give them some idea of what the total may be. Don't let them be surprised by the amount you're charging them for your service. Clients don't need to ever suffer from sticker-shock.

Do a good job. Fix their problem. Exceed their expectations.

Use the principles in this book to guide your relationship with the client. If you do all of that, you're less likely to have a problem with a client. Conflict occurs because one person in the relationship isn't getting what s/he feels s/he should. If your client feels she isn't getting what she should from you, she's going to have an issue with you. Therefore, make sure the client knows you've taken great care of her.

Collect immediately. You can't always do this, but collect money whenever you can in person. As you work with businesses, you may prefer to bill them and they may prefer that too. However, that exposes you to loss. I've lost money simply because I billed the client and then the client went out of business. Once a business is closed, it's virtually impossible to collect those fees.

Bill consistently. If you can't collect money onsite immediately following your service, then bill consistently. That can mean whatever you want it to: bill the day of the service; send out invoices every Friday or on the first, middle or last day of the month. Whatever cycle you create in your office system, stick to it.

Be a follow-up king or queen. Follow-up with the client whether they've paid you or not. Make sure they don't have any additional questions or concerns. Sometimes you'll get another job out of the follow-up, but every time you will reinforce to the client that you care about them, the work you did, and their satisfaction. When a client feels this way, they'll typically pay you without a problem.

Follow your gut about people. If you get a bad feeling, don't do business with them. When you first start doing business with the general public, it may be hard to get a general feeling for who would be a good person to partner with in business in a client/provider relationship. Just as, described throughout this book, you must present yourself as a professional during the interview process, you must become a good interviewer as well. When you start your business or begin your sales career, you think you need to accept every client to survive. That's not true. Keep honing your skills at trusting your gut when it comes to people you're doing business with; when I think of all the people who refused to pay invoices, I am only surprised by a couple of them. The ones I knew would not be good partners told me so through subtle word usage, overall presentation, and uneasy mannerisms. In those cases, I knew immediately I couldn't trust those people. I wish I had trusted my gut. However, by not trusting it, I learned valuable lessons.

Get money up front. Especially for parts. Get all or half of the cost of the parts before you purchase them. There is no need for you to go out of pocket to purchase parts for your clients. The parts needed are the clients' possessions, so let them pay up front. Otherwise, this could happen: you install the parts or software, you invoice the client, and then for some reason out of your control you fail to collect the money. You've essentially bought the parts for the client. Once installed, the parts are hard to get back from the client's property.

Handling Conflicts

§

What do you do when there *is* a problem? Conflicts arise regarding work performed, how much time the job is taking, billing rates, or poor job quality. They can also be over non-work related occurrences, like, say, you break a client's vase. How should you handle the conflict?

Listen. Most people aren't unreasonable. They just want their problem fixed. Let them tell you what they think the unresolved issue is. Really listen. Really try to understand what the client is telling you.

A classic tool in this case is to re-tell what the client is saying to you. Explain the problem as you hear it and ask the client if that's what s/he is saying. If it's not what the client meant, then the client will explain it to you again, perhaps in a better, more understandable way. This shows the client that you really want to understand their issue.

Take Action! By now you fully understand what issue the client is experiencing. Now you have to repair the relationship. If it's something you should have done, take care of it. If it's something you can take care of, then you should do so. If it's something that wasn't covered in your service agreement, then you should explain that fact to her/him, letting them know there will be an additional cost. Most clients won't have a problem with the extra charge, if they understand the task is outside the scope of the work already employed.

A natural response in these situations is to apologize to the client. That's fine, but don't apologize for yourself. I am assuming you're putting all the philosophies in this book to use. If that's the case, you've adopted the concepts of caring about your client, her problem, yourself, your company, and the other core principles explained earlier. If you've really adopted these concepts, then the work you do is excellent. In this case, you don't have to apologize about yourself or the work. Don't say, "I'm sorry." That says you did something wrong or incorrect. Say, "I'm sorry that there was a miscommunication." Or, "I'm sorry you feel that way." However, if you've truly done something wrong or incorrect, admit it and move on. In these cases, you *should* say you're sorry.

Stick to your guns. If you know you did the work properly and completely and you resolved the problems the client faced, don't allow yourself to be bullied when s/he disagrees with you. Some clients are like the big bad wolf. They huff and they puff, but don't let them blow you over. Stick up for yourself. Don't yell, don't be a jerk about it, and don't be ugly at all. Maintain your composure. They'll have a hard time convincing you that you did a poor job, if you know you didn't.

When you explain yourself or your work in these cases, present it like this:

- Be patient. Sometimes conflicts arise because what the client isn't getting from you is knowledge. Clients typically don't understand the work you perform. Sometimes all they want to know is what tasks you performed. Explain it to them but be patient. Explain it a second time in a different way. Don't stop until they get it.

- Talk slowly. Talk slowly with measured words because that will slow down the conflict. It'll slow your heart rate and hopefully your client's heart rate. Without all that blood speeding through your client's veins, maybe the conflict will calm itself, comprehension will occur, and the odds of resolution increase.

- Smile. This is simple. The best way to make anyone

comfortable is to smile, when appropriate and comfortable during the conversation (don't be creepy). Conflict is uncomfortable for reasonable people. You smiling shows you're not trying to make the discomfort worse, and that's good.

Negotiate. Some clients *ARE* unreasonable and will never give in. You should get out of there … with something. The client, at this point, has already decided he won't be calling you again, so you need to end the discussion and leave before the situation gets worse.

Once when I was in this type of situation, I responded, "Listen, I did the work the way it was supposed to have been done. I did the tasks you asked me to perform. However, I want you to be happy, so if you're not happy with the work, then don't pay me."

That was the wrong response.

I should have negotiated. What I should have said is, "I'm sorry you're upset. I performed the tasks we discussed. I communicated with you through the whole process and kept you informed of the progress at every stage, what the obstacles were, and what the next step was going to be. I've checked with your staff as recently as yesterday. They said everything was working fine, so I don't know what the issue is. I'd like to continue working with you to resolve this issue, but I understand you don't want that and don't want to pay the invoice as is. How about this? I'll let you buy the invoice for half price. I've spent 12 hours resolving the described problems and I have to collect something. I did solve these issues: A, B, and C; so that's worth something."

This allows the client to "win" and you get something for your time. You cannot afford to work for free.

Follow-up. I know. I know. He basically stole half the invoice amount from you, when you deserved 100% of your billed time. As bitter as this may make you feel to do, you should send a handwritten card a few days later to the client. Tell him that you appreciated the opportunity to work with him. Tell him your aim is always to exceed your clients' expectations, and you are sorry he felt the situation wasn't satisfactory.

Don't tell him if another problem arises you'd like to help him ... because you don't want that. You shouldn't want that.

When building a business, people often think they have to accept every job or project that comes their way. Truthfully, though, a client like this will waste your time, even if he pays half of the invoice. The pattern will continue forever. He'll always be trouble. Cut him loose.

However, by following-up with him, you may pour water on his fire, putting it out. This is the kind of guy that will talk bad about you to other people. If you send a follow-up note to him, it may calm him down. If he's calm, then he may not provide negative word of mouth reviews. That's the goal of the follow-up note.

Notes

§

Before delving into the next ideas, methods, philosophies, principles, and best practices, examine again each of the Core Principles again. Write down any ideas of your own in relation to the ideas presented here. How do they apply to your job? To your client interactions? Do you agree or disagree with the principles presented? Use this examination as a conversation started, either with your staff or your manager or your business's owner.

_____

_____

_____

_____

_____

_____

_____

_____

_____

_____

Part Four: Phone

While phones have evolved into critical tools of business, they also can get in the way of building relationships. There are hundreds of articles published about how phones may be damaging all types of relationships, not just business relationships.

In this section, you can learn some simple tricks, and important reasons, to help you detach your phone from your hand, if you want to build a professional relationship with your clients. The ideas are basic, but if implemented, they can have monumentally positive impacts on your budding or established relationships (personal and professional).

Phone: Receiving Calls

Massage Your Message

§

Again, first impressions. They're so important. They can make or break a business relationship or even a personal relationship. There are hundreds of scenarios where first impressions occur. One of the most common scenarios in this age of phonebooks *(yes, they still exist)*, websites, and referral groups is via incoming phone calls.

You can't be expected to answer every incoming call. When you're with a client, staff member, or anyone else, you *shouldn't* answer the phone. Therefore, creating a professional voicemail is a critical component to your perceived professionalism. It may be the sole introductory opportunity between you/your company and a potential new client.

Creating a Voicemail Greeting. Having a good voicemail greeting is important. You are a professional service provider. That's what you do. That's how you need to present yourself to the world. That's why people are calling you, so your greeting should reflect your professionalism.

1. Environmental Aspects of Creating a Voicemail Greeting
    - Don't record it while driving your car with the windows down.
    - Don't record it while driving your car with the air conditioning/heat set at full blast.
    - Record the greeting in a quiet room. A well-insulated room (no tile) to avoid echo and the chamber effect.
2. Planning Your Greeting

- Write down the greeting on a piece of paper. Type it on your computer.
- Practice reading it repeatedly until it sounds like your regular conversational cadence and phrasing. It should sound like you're talking, not reading the greeting.
- When it's time to record the greeting, read it off your paper or computer.

3. What the Greeting Should Be
- Thank the person for calling.
- Give your name.
- Give a brief reason why you're not answering your phone.
- Invite the caller to leave you a voicemail.
- Then provide an expectation for when they will get a callback.
- Close the message with another word of thanks or some pleasantry.

4. Post-Checking Your Greeting
- After you record it, listen to it to make sure you spoke clearly and that you didn't sound like you're reading.
- Are there noises in the background? A crying child? A siren. A dog barking? Did your computer make a noise during the recording? Did the doorbell ring or someone knock on the door? Is there a radio or the TV playing in the background?
- Can you hear anything in the message that may distract the caller or will present you in a less than professional manner?

If you have doubt about the way you sound or the noises in the background, then record it again. Keep doing it until you know whoever calls you will be happy with the greeting. Have three friends listen to it and critique it, if you don't trust your own judgment.

Leaving a Voicemail Message. At the other end of the message spectrum is what you say when you call someone and the call goes to voicemail. On the television show *Seinfeld*, there was a great episode *(every episode was great, for the record)* named "The Phone Message" where the character George leaves a poorly structured message on a woman's answering machine. (*It was really, really bad.*) The episode progresses until he attempts to steal the answering machine tape, so the woman never hears the message.

We've all left messages like that! All in all, though, it's not a terrible crime. Completely forgivable. Completely unnecessary. Here are some tips to leave a voicemail that won't embarrass you.

Know the expectations. The most likely expectation when you call someone is one of two outcomes: the person will answer your call and speak to you, or the call will go to voicemail. You should be prepared for both possibilities. These steps can work for both circumstances.

Call when it's best for you. You're dialing the number, so you know who you're calling, why you're calling that person, and even when you're calling. If it's not the best time to call for you, don't call at that moment. Instead, opt for a time when you're secluded in a calm, quiet, and private spot to make the call.

Breathe and beat fear. These terrible voicemail messages we leave usually involve some sort of nervousness, fear, or anxiety. To avoid them, perform these two exercises to calm yourself before calling.

- While sitting in a quiet environment, take 10 deep breaths, slowly exhaling and keeping your eyes closed. As you exhale, relax your stomach. As you progress through the 10 breaths, you should feel your muscle tension relax. Your shoulders should slump slightly, and you should have an overall sense of relaxation.

- Fear is built on anxiety. Humans focus on their fears, and as they're focused on, the fears become bigger than they actually are. A tool to counter this is to break down the situation to its simplest form. All you're doing is calling someone. Before you actually dial the number, just repeat to yourself about 30 times (or as many times as it takes) the following statement: "I'm just calling a person. I'm just calling a person. I'm just calling a person." No matter *why* you're calling, you are simply calling a *person*.

There's no stuttering in voicemails. Whether you speak to the person or are leaving a message, planning what you want to say can help, and it really only takes a moment of slowing down and jotting a few notes on paper. Preparing like this most likely results in you not stuttering, not repeating words or sentences, not speaking too quickly, and/or not communicating with verbal pauses like "Um."

Ask yourself these questions:

- Why am I calling this person?
- Is there a call to action on the recipient's part, or am I just giving information?
- What do I want to get out of this phone call?

Then write down the voicemail you'd like to leave.

A voicemail example: "Hi, Mr. Smith, this is Mary Sugarman, calling in reference to the job posting on your company's web site for Administrative Assistant. I am very interested in speaking with you about this opportunity. My phone number is 555-555-5555. Please return my call at your convenience. Again, my name is Mary Sugarman, and my number is 555-555-5555. Thanks so much. Have a nice day."

And, if he answers the phone, you can still use part of your voicemail message. "Hi, Mr. Smith, this is Mary Sugarman. I am calling in reference to the job posting on your company's web site for Administrative Assistant. Do you have a moment to discuss that position with me?"

The result of either of these scenarios is that Mr. Smith understands you speak professionally and clearly, as well as knowing you communicate with purpose and a collected thought process. That means you won't be George, trying to concoct a scheme to delete the message you just left.

Phone: Returning Calls

Phone-iquette: Returning Calls

§

While it's important to let your phone go to voicemail, silence it, and ignore it when you're with a client, it's also important to stay in constant contact with your clients.

Here's what I mean: don't be rude with your phone usage in front of a client or while a client is paying you; however, as soon as you're finished with that client, listen to voicemail, and make return calls.

Some appointments take an hour, some longer. Doesn't matter. Your voicemail greeting should reflect that you're with a client and will return the call as soon as possible. The key is making the return call.

The best practice is returning the call within an hour.

With the options presented by today's technology, you can have:

Voicemail. Voicemail is convenient. Quickly accessible. Usually it can be checked with a passcode by you or an assistant. One option is to have your assistant call your voicemail every hour on the hour. S/He takes notes on the messages left by your clients. Then, your assistant calls each client who left a voicemail and lets them know you're with a client but will return the call shortly. Most clients will be understanding. To a large degree, once you've established your relationship with the client, your clients will just need acknowledgement of the receipt of their problem.

Voicemail translation. There are numerous tools that will transcribe your voicemails and text them to your phone or send them to your email account. While sometimes imperfect in its translation, you typically will decipher the idea of the message. I personally hate listening to voicemail. I would let my assistant listen to messages and tell me who I need to call. However, when I have the translation feature turned on, I check via text or email before I drive away from my last meeting. I quickly know who I need to call and who my assistant can call. Usually the ones I need to call are ones that need information that only I have or who have a higher priority of a problem. The ones I allow my assistant to call are ones who want to schedule something, which I can't do while driving.

Call-forwarding. If you're going to be busy for an extended period of time and you won't be able to listen to your voicemails or check emails and texts for multiple hours, then forward your phone to your office receptionist, dispatcher, secretary, or assistant. Forward it to anyone who can talk to the client or who can respond to the client in an appropriate amount of time.

All of these options communicate to your client their importance to you. That's critical to building a relationship with them. Your clients don't know how to do something, they are humbling themselves to ask for help, and they're willing to pay you for the assistance; the least you can do is show them you care about them and their problems.

Get Beyond The Gatekeeper

§

"She's away from her desk, may I take a message?"

"No, she's not home."

Gatekeepers!

Time is a commodity. I mean, that's usually what professional service providers are selling anyway (along with knowledge). It's valuable ... to both you and your clients, so why get stuck behind the gate? Gatekeepers are tasked with saving their bosses or higher-ups from taking part in unwanted conversations over the phone; they're tasked with helping their bosses and higher-ups save their own time for billable hours. They lock out people on purpose from reaching the decision-makers. Bust down the gate with this simple rule.

Announce yourself.

Don't make the gatekeeper ask, "May I say who is calling?" or "May I tell her who is calling?"

Instead, I find this works quite well: "Hi, this is Mike Sullivan from Window Tinting, Inc., returning Mary Beth's phone call about her car's windows. May I speak with her please?"

If the person answering the phone gives you his/her name, then use that. "Hi, Sherry, this is Mike Sullivan from Window Tinting, Inc., returning Mary Beth's phone call about her car's windows. May I speak with her please?"

Let's break down that greeting.

"Hi, Sherry..."

You engage the receptionist in a personal level by greeting her.

"…this is Mike Sullivan from Window Tinting, Inc."

You announce who you are and the company you're with. This identifies you as an authority.

"…returning Mary Beth's phone call…"

You let the gatekeeper know that you are participating in a known, ongoing conversation with Mary Beth, who most likely is expecting the return call.

You use Mary Beth's first name, which shows familiarity.

"…about her car's windows."

You tell the receptionist why you're calling. This shows her the importance of the call.

"May I speak with her please?"

Then you graciously ask the receptionist to let you through the gate in order to connect with Mary Beth. This empowers the receptionist to grant you the passage, which makes her feel a little more in control the situation.

Usually the gatekeeper will connect you with the target.

However, sometimes you may be put on hold while the receptionist contacts the target, or in this case, Mary Beth. You've given the receptionist a good reason for her to interrupt the target. If you hadn't supplied a reason, then the receptionist wouldn't put you on hold. Therefore, by reaching this point of being on hold, you can feel confident that if you're told the target is unavailable, then she probably is. You can also feel confident that you'll get a call back.

I do not recommend this for cold calling. That's not what this book is about.

Remember, gatekeepers aren't just at your professional client's offices. They're also at your clients' homes.

Many of my clients were females, and I often had to call their homes to discuss with them a work issue. If their husbands answered the phone, I announced to them who I was, the company I represented, to whom I needed to speak, and why I needed to speak with his wife.

"Hi, this is Mike Sullivan from Windows Tinting, Inc. Mrs. Smith asked me to call her to give her an update on her car's work status. May I speak with her please?"

With this approach, you've made sure the husband isn't suspicious of a man calling his wife at home and he knows you're not a telemarketer, so he'll allow you through the gate.

The objective here is to maintain appropriate, timely communication with your clients. That type of communication fosters trust, relationship building, and importance of the two-way communication. Keeping this type of communication consistent will allow you to continue getting beyond the gatekeepers, as well as maintaining a profitable, professional relationship with your client.

Phone: Onsite Call Protocol

Their Phone Call Is More Important Than You

§

After being permitted beyond the receptionist, you will find yourself entering the office of the busy user who needs your help. There may need to be one last sentence typed on an email before you can take over. There may be a "Save" to a document needed before you take over. There could be any number of things the user has to do before you take over. But, if the user is on the phone when you step into the doorway, give the user privacy.

Just wave and smile and then step back into the hallway and out of sight. The user will know you are there and will hurry the phone call. However, you won't be hovering over her/him, making the situation more tense and unnerving.

When the client hangs up the call, you can step back into the doorway and start the interaction over.

If you are with a client and they need to take a call, then you should step out of the room and give her/him privacy. At least, sincerely offer to leave the room. Stay close, and when the phone call has ended, re-enter the room.

This activity informs the client you know and respect the boundaries of your relationship. This builds your client's view of your trustworthiness and professionalism.

Smartphones Can Kill A Relationship

§

When a client is paying me, she/he deserves my full attention. Period. I limit my distractions when I am with a client. That includes, for example, purging stress before seeing a client, not being hungry when I am with a client, not having to use the rest room, and not being tired during the meeting or appointment. But, mostly it includes not using my smartphone during a client's time with me.

Seriously. No phone usage.

My biggest issue with the phone is taking a call while with a client. I hate this! I've preached this to every employee I had who interacted with clients onsite. Do not take a call (from a family member or another client) while you're with a client. One client should not pay you to talk on the phone with another one. Even if you need to take the call, don't interrupt a discussion with a client to do so.

It's rude to work on Client B's issue at the same time you're in Client A's office or home, even if you're willing to remove the time you spoke on the phone from the Client A's invoice; even if it's a quick call and you're just going to tell Client B you will call them back; even if you're alone in Client A's office. There's no non-emergency reason to take any call in this situation.

Taking the call is rude and unprofessional. It shows you

don't care about the client and her/his issue. It shows at that moment someone else matters more to you than your paying client. No, that can't ever be true.

Rude behavior will kill your relationship with your client.

Turn off your ringer. Silence your phone. Not hearing a phone call will limit your distraction level. Same for incoming texts, calendar appointments and so on.

Don't check social media pages.

Don't read the news.

Don't play any games.

Don't fidget with it.

Heck, leave it in the car.

Seriously! Your Phone Will Ruin You

§

Cell phones have seemingly become an extension of our bodies. If you go to a restaurant and see a couple eating dinner together, usually one or both of them will be using their phone rather than talking to each other. I even had a cashier at the grocery store once using her cell phone while she was scanning up my groceries. They've become an instrument to assist humans in filling up times of boredom, in addition to their professional benefit. So, naturally, humans have taken the convenience too far, and now there are rules to manage how we use our cell phones.

Conventional wisdom lists these cell phone best practices:

- Don't text while driving;
- Don't talk on the phone when you're at the checkout or placing a food order;
- Don't talk too loud in public;
- Don't wear your Bluetooth earpiece when you're not on a call; and
- Don't employ annoying ringtones.

I'd like to add a few to that list.

How will you answer the phone? I had a friend that answered his cell phone calls with: "Go." One time I heard him answer the phone and say, "Speak." But usually is was "Go." That didn't exactly warm the hearts of the people on the other end of the phone. He was in a high-pressure, high-dollar position. He wasn't dealing with the general public; he was dealing with just his staff. That doesn't make it right though. I know much more "important" people in much higher pressure positions dealing with a greater amount of money than my friend had been, and they answered their phone calls cordially.

One of your tasks, before your next incoming phone call, is to decide how you're going to answer your phone. Or, you need to decide how your staff is going to answer their next incoming phone call. Either way, it's important.

Why is it important? Answering that question assumes one thing: you want to portray your company and yourself as providing high quality, high level service. Imagine the next incoming call is a potential client. That client has enough work that your income will triple. They're looking for a service-oriented vendor to fill their need. Now, how are you going to answer that call? "Go." "Speak." I don't think so. That potential client wants to hear a pleasant, happy, helpful (professional) voice answer the phone.

Every call should be answered just as happily and helpfully as the hypothetical incoming call described above. Even a small, new client should be treated the same as the one who would triple your income. Returning clients *most definitely* should be treated as if they're the best people in the world. *Because they are!* It's easier to keep a client you already have than to gain a new one. So, don't answer the phone with anything less than this: "Thanks for calling <Company Name>. This is <Name>. How can I help you?"

Background noises are deafening. Today's cell phones are so technologically advanced you can take them to a concert and record the band playing. It sounds relatively good when you play it back the next day. However, if you're talking on the phone while the band is playing, the phone gets confused about what sound it should be focusing on. So, the person on the other end is getting an earful, literally. Probably nearly deaf after that call. Candy wrappers are loud for the person on the other end of your phone. Other people talking, nearby cars and motorcycles, paper rattling, stapling paper, and opening a squeaky door, for example, are all terribly loud on the other end of the phone connection. Be aware of where you are and how it may sound to the person you're speaking with on your phone. I once said to a person I was speaking with, "Where are you? You sound like you're at a construction site." All she was doing was wheeling the garbage can to the road and getting the mail. My ears are still recovering!

Ringer off. No Vibration. One key to building business relationships is to demonstrate to your client that they are important. That means concentrating on them, whether you're talking to or working for them. The best way to show this is to turn your cell phone ringer volume to silent (not even on vibrate). Turn the ringer silent during:

- Service calls
- Meetings
- Business lunches
- Business dinners
- When someone enters your office
- At business networking events
- When you're in the car with a client or staff member
- Anytime you are working for a client in their house or office

When you are deep in business conversation with a client, a cell phone ringing acts only as a distraction and irritant. Perhaps to you, but most definitely to the client. It changes the focus of your interaction. Even if you don't answer the call, you have to stop what you are doing, fumble with your phone, and press the Reject button. Then you have to get re-focused. Worst case, you let the phone ring until it goes to voicemail. And that's distracting! The ringing demands your attention, which should be focused on the person you're with.

What happens if you don't answer the phone when you're with someone? They leave a voicemail. They don't leave a voicemail. You see their missed call notice in your call log and you call them back later. They see you're not answering and send you a text. They call back later. None of these things is so terrible that you should interrupt the business conversation in which you are currently involved.

The table is for food. Riding the coattails of the above section's theme of distraction, leaving your cell phone on the lunch or dinner table during a meeting is a no-no. Even with the volume turned down, the screen illuminates and you see who is calling. *Distraction!* You start thinking about what that person calling needs from you, instead of paying attention to the person you're with or job you're doing.

Perhaps it's the office calling. *I wonder what fire they want me to put out now!* Perhaps a client who only calls when there is an emergency. *Their emergency is going to change my whole afternoon schedule.* Maybe it's your child's school. *I hope nothing is wrong.* Maybe it's your spouse. *I told her this morning I had an important lunch; so why would she call me during that important lunch?* Maybe it's your aging parents. *Gosh, I hope everyone is all right.* Perhaps it's your lawyer or accountant. *What now? Is the IRS auditing me? Who's suing me today?*

Holy cow! I forgot I was at lunch with someone! What were we talking about?

Stow away the phone. In your pocket. On the seat next to you. Leave it in the car! The only person that's important is the one you're with. (And take that advice for your personal life too. Having dinner with your spouse? Pay attention to her/him. Put your phone down. S/He will be thrilled to have your undivided attention!) Besides that, there is nothing anyone can be contacting you for that can't wait 30 minutes until your lunch is over. I mean, what are you going to do about it right then anyway? Your child is sick at school. *All right. Your child is still at school, comfortably positioned in a cot, I would presume. S/He is fine.* A client calling. *No client can realistically expect you are available 24/7 at any moment of the day. You deserve to eat.* Your spouse is calling. *I once received a call during an appointment solely to be asked where the reset button was located on the garbage disposal.*

Is that worth interrupting an important conversation with a client?

I've met business owners who want to answer every call that comes in. No voicemail. And that's great! For the person who is calling. Not for the person you are with. It may show your dedication to your job and clients, but it also shows a lack of common courtesy. I called a client and he answered the call. He said, "I'm doing an estimate with a customer. Can I call you back?" Wait, you're with a client, at her house, and you're trying to convince her to pay you … and you took my call?! **No!** There is nothing more important at that moment than giving your client attention and getting that job. Don't answer your phone!

Keep some things private. In particular, don't argue with your staff, spouse, children, or anyone else via cell phone in public. It's unbecoming. Of all parties involved. Everyone knows arguments occur, but arguments are private. All parties should be able to contain themselves until they are at home, alone in a car, or in a closed conference room at the office.

I have witnessed phone calls between staff members and their spouses where the spouse who called immediately launched into a tirade about whatever was bothering her. There was no regard for what the spouse was working on, where the spouse was at the time, or who the spouse was with at the moment.

My son recently told me after walking our dog that he'd seen a couple in their front yard arguing. The wife was yelling, "Look at me! Look at me! Why did you say that? What's wrong with you?"

In their front yard!

Feet from their front door!

Just go inside already…

People should be able to control themselves long enough to get inside the house before they raise their concerns and voices. Now those neighbors will always be the front yard yellers to us. In my opinion, it's not a sign of a healthy person who can't control their emotions or who can't stop themselves from lashing out immediately when angered or hurt.

Why embarrass yourself and other people around you by engaging in an argument in public? No one wins, but you definitely lose.

I don't want to hear your conversation. Whether it be confidential business or a personal conversation or argument, I don't want to hear it. Nor do I need to hear it. Volume on cell phones can go very high now. Some people keep the in-call volume so high that people around them can hear both sides of the conversation. Turn it down. Then, if you feel you *must* take a personal call around other people, at least they won't hear the full content of the call.

Notes

§

Before delving into the next ideas, methods, philosophies, principles, and best practices, examine again each of the Core Principles again. Write down any ideas of your own in relation to the ideas presented here. How do they apply to your job? To your client interactions? Do you agree or disagree with the principles presented? Use this examination as a conversation started, either with your staff or your manager or your business's owner.

_____

_____

_____

_____

_____

_____

_____

_____

_____

_____

Part Five:
Interpersonal Skills

If you're the book that's judged by your cover (Appearance), then the topics in this section are your book's contents. Appearances don't tell the whole story, but they are accompanied and furthered by your behavior. Business professionals who strive to create and maintain client relationships have to continually impress their clients with loyalty, commitment, thoughtfulness, and service, which are four things most companies and technicians can do. That's why this section is so important. It gets to the human side of doing business, which is something not most companies and technicians can do. Conducting yourself in the ways outlined herein can win you honest and genuine clients for years. Remember, these topics don't have much to do with your professional skills; they have to do with your ability to connect with people, which is the foundation of every relationship.

Interpersonal Skills: Soft Skills

Southern Hospitality Works Well

§

In some parts of the country, using "ma'am" and "sir" to address women and men, respectively, isn't the norm, but there's no reason it shouldn't be.

Some women object to being called "ma'am" because they think it means they are old.

I don't know any men that object to being referred to as "sir."

Saying "Yes, ma'am" is a sign of respect. People say it to older women and to younger women. There isn't really any differentiation anymore. It's a term used to portray respect from one person to a woman.

The same goes for "Yes, sir." Respect. What man doesn't want that? You display immediate respect for a man when you call him "sir." It's not just for older men or more powerful men. It's for males of all ages, like ma'am is for women. In fact, I call my son "sir" all of the time.

You don't have to say it at the end of every sentence, like in the military. However, if you use it strategically, then it displays sincerely your respect for the person (as a person) to whom you are talking. What that does is immediately establish you as a professional service provider who inherently respects people. Furthermore, the client subconsciously receives the message from you that you respect her/him. And, that will get you the job over another candidate who doesn't portray respect for the person.

Imagine you and a competitor go into a potential client's business for a sales presentation. Your prices, services, and guarantees are exactly the same. However, you use words (ma'am/sir) that show respect for the person as a person, but your competitor doesn't. You'll earn the client over your competitor!

I contend that clients want to be serviced by people who care about them, their business or their families, and their respective goals. Expressing genuine common courtesy and respect will play a part in the client's overall impression of you. And who do you represent? Your company. Your displays of genuine respect transfer for the client to your company. If you have respect for the client, his business, and his goals of the business, then so will your company.

It works.

Handling women's objections to being called ma'am. My parents forced me and my brothers to use ma'am/sir throughout our childhood. It's been so ingrained in me that I don't even know when I am doing it. I have been asked not to use "ma'am" by female clients many times. "Please don't call me ma'am." I almost always instinctively reply, "Yes, ma'am."

"You did it again!" They usually protest.

"Sorry. I will try to not use it, but as a sign of respect for women I like, it just comes out automatically. I'll give you my mom's number, and you can call her to complain about it. It's her fault I use it."

I've never had a woman continue to ask me to stop using it after that explanation.

You're The Priest And The Therapist

§

People say too much. Ask someone a Yes-or-No question, and you're likely to get a paragraph/essay answer. Add the feeling of comfort to that inclination, and you'll be shocked at what people tell you. When you go into another person's comfort zone (home or office), the person feels comfortable … even if you're a stranger. Comfort breeds familiarity.

I've been told of pornography addictions, marriage problems, violence, as well as child issues and pregnancy troubles. I even found a couple smoking marijuana in their garage while I worked on their home PC. *(I guess they couldn't wait until I left!)*

On one hand, what a compliment! I'd represented myself in such a way that people felt comfortable around me. They trusted me. They knew I'd maintain their confidentiality. They respected me. In some cases, they thought I could help them with their problems. On the other hand, maybe they were just happy to have had a friendly ear. Most of the time, the content of these exchanges were pretty mundane, although every now and then the information was uncomfortable.

As you plan for the relationships this book will assist you in creating, keep this section locked away in the back of your mind because …

This will eventually happen to you. Perhaps not every day, but it will happen. When it does happen, don't be too surprised. Although every time it happens to me, I still am a little surprised. Maybe I'm naïve and go into each of these situations with a high level of professionalism, I don't know. I'm still surprised though when a housewife tells me what a jerk her husband is or when a husband slams his phone down after an angry call with his wife.

Control your reaction. Don't looked horrified when you hear something of this nature. The client isn't telling you her/his secrets simply because you're a trustworthy individual. Sometimes they think you'll find out anyway, so they just tell you. Your job is to react professionally and cast no judgment. Listen. Smile and nod. Acknowledge the information in some way then move on.

Fix the problem. I was once at a client's home. The family's daughter was in a special schooling program. She needed a laptop, but she needed the wireless capabilities removed. Simple enough. However, the mother told me much more information about the situation. I heard all about the school, why the daughter was there, how the mother reacted initially to the problem, and so on. I expressed parental sympathy, said I'd keep the family in my prayers, and then I solved the problem by removing the wireless card completely. Done. Mom had her dignity and relief; daughter had a usable laptop for her purposes; and I participated in a relationship I built.

Don't fix the problem. One of the things I like to do during an initial visit with a client is to find personal items in their office or home and use that item as a conversation starter. This creates the foundation for a relationship. Once I saw a framed photograph of an old boat on a client's wall. I was struck by the photograph because of the brilliant blue coloring in the water, the sky, and the boat's paint. When I asked about the photo, the client told me a marvelous story about growing up on that boat for a few years with his dad. The client was able to tell the story of what was clearly a good memory. I gained an opportunity to learn something about the client. And we've communicated well ever since. The same can be done with items on someone's desk. I asked one lady about a handmade ashtray on her desk. Her daughter made it in elementary school. Wonderful stories began wonderful relationships.

However, this can also turn over some ugly information. On one woman's wall was a photograph of her husband at the finish line of a marathon. The medal he won that day was draped over the top, right corner of the frame. I asked about it. What she told me was a horrifying story of her controlling husband. It was an unexpected turn in what had been an otherwise delightful first visit. I said to her, "Well, then I won't ask any more questions about him. Can you show me again what you were doing when the error occurred on the screen?" She laughed and demonstrated the process for me. I lightened the mood, let her know I listened and understood what she was saying about her husband, and then re-focused the conversation/relationship back to the reason I was there in the first place. She seemed to appreciate each of those aspects of my response.

I couldn't fix that problem she conveyed. Perhaps I felt bad for her. Maybe I instantly decided to dislike the husband. Whatever my emotional response, I couldn't fix that problem. So I didn't try. There was no comment I could make that would make the situation go away. However, any comment I made could've resulted in a worsening of the situation. It was best to move on.

Remember the client's reveal and follow up, if/when appropriate. When I was told of the family's daughter having trouble which resulted in her new schooling, I discreetly asked how it was going the next time I saw the mother. She was delighted to inform me all was well. She even thanked me again for helping with the laptop, then she gave me a hug for being concerned about her and her family. When I saw the woman with the controlling husband a second time, I did not bring him up. I didn't remind her even that she told me about him. Why should I? It might make her uncomfortable. And I didn't want to bring that type of discomfort into our professional relationship.

Interpersonal Skills: Onsite Decorum

Whose Chair Is It?

§

As an IT consultant, I'd find that business clients were often experiencing halted progress until I arrived to fix their computer. Whatever task they needed to do was hampered by the computer's inability to function properly, which resulted in lost productivity time. They'd be so excited when I arrived that the first thing they'd do was jump right out of their chair, getting out of my way immediately. The sooner I was in the chair and working on their computer, the sooner they could get back to work.

This became the norm, and then one day I found myself being impatient because a client wasn't getting out of my way fast enough. I realized this was the wrong attitude. It wasn't my chair. It was their chair.

As a resolution to this situation, I instituted a personal policy that became a business rule for my technicians. Similar to asking permission to enter someone's home, I would ask permission to sit in someone's chair.

"Do you mind if I sit?"

"May I switch places with you?"

"When you get to a stopping point, may I have your seat?"

This shows respect for the person's space. It also sets the stage for them to not be vulnerable. You are coming into their office and taking control of it. Asking their permission lets them know you know whose office it is. That's a good thing.

Now, be prepared for a smart-aleck answer, like, "Well, how else will you work on my problem."

Just smile and sit when the client exits the chair. It isn't about her/his answer to your question. Aside from showing respect and asking permission, you are kindly asking them to move out of your way. They will, so it doesn't matter if they answer you or not, or what their answer is. Most are working and not thinking about your needs. Most will apologize for not realizing you need their space and will promptly move.

Commentary Is About You, Not Your Work

§

Where I live, it isn't hard to find someone who knows another person I know. If you're building business relationships properly and effectively, then you'll know a bunch of people and a greater bunch of people will know you. Therefore, never talk about other people. You never know how the person you're talking to, with, or about is connected to other people. You could be talking about their sibling, parent, cousin, gym workout partner, best friend, or best friend's boyfriend/girlfriend.

If you're providing a professional service and are building relationships properly, then you will get to know all the people at each business client's office. There could be personality conflicts at that business. There most likely is, so don't give commentary about other people, what they look like, how they think or talk, or what decisions they've made.

That puts you in the gossip line and not in the professional service line.

I often tell clients, "I'm in the consulting business, not the commentary business."

Gossiping turns your professional presence into one of "please like me." That's not professional, and there is no place for that in this type of professional relationship.

Keep Your Mouth Shut

§

In the IT world, there have been a great number of news articles describing how PC technicians have stolen images of clients from their computers, laptops, and smartphones. These articles have shaken the public trust in the people who serve their IT needs. That shaken trust is a black cloud over the whole IT professional service industry. One bad apple spoils the bunch, right?

As an IT professional, I had to fight that inherent distrust every day, as well as sell myself, my skills, my business brand, my services, and my own ethics. It makes every IT service provider's job even more difficult when these incidents of fractured trust occur.

Therefore, I made it a blanket rule in my business that no client details ever be revealed. I shied away from advertising with my clients' names. I didn't give away the manner in which people lived or what I saw on their computers, and their data always stayed protected.

If a client lives in what I would consider filth, then it never mattered and I didn't talk about it. The fact is that person has the right to live how s/he wants. Why should it bother me? She needs my help with something. Everyone needs help. She's just like you and me. She has to stay there when the job is done, and I get to go home to live the way I want to live. If I'm dictated by the ideas in this book, then this won't matter.

Some clients have private pictures on their PC. It's their PC. It's their data. Just because I was working on their PC, it didn't mean I was invited to view and keep their private pictures.

Some industries are governed by HIPAA and other privacy and confidentiality laws. If your industry isn't governed as such, make up your own confidentiality rules. Over time your rules can become part of your marketing, as well as your reputation.

I live in a city where it seems everyone knows everything about everyone, and I have seen major business transactions derail because one of the parties broke confidentiality. Secrets leak. Deals fall apart. Reputations are tarnished. Personal respect is lost on all sides.

The best policy is to do your job with ethics, integrity, and respect for your client.

The following text is directly from my business's web site in regard to this topic.

> In July, 2012, a news article circulated about a big-box store's employee stealing compromising photos off a customer's smart phone. CompuMend, Inc. President, Chris Wendel, responded to that as such:
>
> "This is why [the article subject outlined above] for your IT/computer needs (business or personal) you need a consultant and not a PC tech repairman. A consultant, by my definition, is someone who is on your side. There is an inherent confidentiality in working with a consultant. The training materials in the company I own include in its definition of the word consultant passages about protecting the client, protecting the client's data, and being an advocate for the client, as well as maintaining strict client privacy practices. I'd like to implore everyone to really think about whom you're letting assist you with your IT/computer needs."

This philosophy has enabled me to build a reputation and a brand of trust with my clients.

Maintain confidentiality with your clients' information—finding out how that relates to your business and industry isn't something I can help with in this format, but there is a need for confidentiality in your business and industry. Set the standard. You're being trusted by your client. Keep that trust. Fight for them to maintain their privacy. Be their advocate for security and privacy.

Say "No" To Food

§

Living in a region known for its southern hospitality, being welcomed like family into someone's home is common. A favorite polite offering by people in these situations is food and drink. On the bright side, this displays your client's manners, as well as her/his thoughtfulness toward others and possibly her/his respect for you as a person and professional. On the other hand, it can come back to haunt you by hurting your long-term relationship with the client.

I had a strict rule with my technicians to never accept food and drink from a client. Each technician knew the rule, but only one ignored it. One time. One time was all it took for him to figure out why it wasn't permitted. He was working through the lunch hour and was going to be at the client's home for another couple of hours. The client offered him some homemade potato salad. He accepted. He told me he took a quick break from working and ate with her at the kitchen table. "I was hungry," he told me. "I deducted the time from her bill."

Two weeks later the client called, unhappy with the result of one of the tasks the technician performed. She protested, "I even gave him lunch!"

She used the lunch as a tool against him and my company. I'm sure at the time she fed my technician she was just being nice. She was feeding a man who was working hard on her behalf. Later it turned into a sore spot for her and an additional reason for her to be upset.

A quick meal or drink isn't worth the personal cost of having a client complain, "I fed him at the same table I feed my children!"

Breakfast. If you have a 9 AM appointment, drink your coffee before you get there. Bring your own coffee if you need to, but don't accept a cup from the client. Eat breakfast before you arrive; don't eat it while you're there (even if you bring it with you). Quite simply, don't accept a pastry or other food from a client in their home or office. The exception is that you've planned on a working breakfast. In these cases, use your best table manners.

Lunch. If you're working through the lunch hour, bring mints with you. The stimulation of the mints in your mouth will fool your body into thinking you're eating, then get food after you finish the job. Another option is to take a break and run to a sandwich shop, for example, where you can eat and return to the project quickly. No business client will object to you getting life-sustaining food. Although, home users are different. If you're onsite in the middle of the day, the home client may have made special arrangements to be there at the same time. You shouldn't leave a home client's house in order to get lunch. You should have eaten before you had arrived at the house. Plan ahead or use the mint trick.

Additionally, if the client offers to have your lunch brought in, then they are more concerned with getting the job done than they are of your need to eat. Don't accept. Just finish the work and get out of there. If the client offers to take you to lunch, then they *are* concerned about you eating. Still, don't go. Keep working and get out of there. Go for your own lunch. Eat a mint.

The objective here is to not provide the client any ammunition to shoot at you if they became unhappy with your service, response time, or other service factor. For example, let them call you and say they need you to come back out because something isn't right with their system. This call example is a request or a complaint. Don't let them call and say that they fed you, thinking you'd take better care of them, but their system is still broken. This call is a personal affront to the client's hospitality, kindness, and character.

Don't get me wrong. Eating with a client is fine; just don't do it while you're working to resolve a problem for a client, unless the problem is a long ongoing issue, where the lunch can be used as a status update session. Another use of the business meal is to gather information on a pending project. However, you shouldn't stop work on fixing a client's air conditioning unit or the client's server to attend lunch with the client. Save an engaging, social lunch for another day, like after you've saved the day by repairing the server and returning the productivity to the client's business.

Dinner. After business hours is covered later in the book.

Respect The Competition

§

You don't have to like your competition, but you do need to respect them. And your industry.

For example, there are always multiple ways of doing the same thing. You prefer your way, I prefer mine, and they prefer their way. Do they all get the job done? Most likely. That means, you shouldn't develop ill-feelings toward your competition just because they do things their way and not your way.

However, businesses change service providers quite a bit. Some businesses try multiple service providers before they settle on one long relationship. Others never settle on one relationship. Some change service providers after a multi-year relationship with one company. There are many reasons clients change their providers.

The reason's I've heard over the years are:

- "That company was nickel-and-diming me."
- "The service grew slower over time."
- "We never saw the technicians anymore."
- "We didn't know what they were doing for us."
- "The only communication we received from them was an invoice."
- "They never called me back."
- "They grew too fast."
- "They didn't know what they were doing."
- "They weren't friendly."
- "The quality of service slacked over time."

- "I stopped trusting them."

I'm sure anyone who's been in business for any length of time has heard some or all of these reasons, and they've probably heard other reasons as well.

Since businesses are constantly changing their service providers, one task a service provider has to master is taking over a client from another service vendor. This is where that "respect" plays a part in how you conduct yourself. Taking over a client from another service provider can be a delicate high-wire act, but it's an important one. If you navigate this properly, then you could be headed in the direction of establishing a long relationship with this client, which is the goal of this exercise, as well as everything you do every day. Here are tips on how to walk that wire:

- **Don't bad-mouth the competition's reputation.** This is never a good idea. Remember, you never know who the person you're talking to knows. You don't know the type of relationship the person has with your competition. The old rule of not saying a word if you don't have anything nice to say is a great rule. When you bad-mouth your competitor, you:

  a. Look shallow and petty (damages you/your company)

  b. Come across as desperate (damages you/your company)

  c. Set the stage for you to be perfect, and you won't be perfect; you know you're not perfect and so does the client (damages you/your company)

  No one wants to do business with a provider who seems awkward, desperate, or petty. They want knowledgeable, confident, and fair providers.

- **Don't accuse the competition of doing the wrong thing in the wrong way.** I have found that the business world has a way of building cynicism. People dump into these businesses, at least, their lives, families, marriages, and savings. It becomes personal to them. When one of these business owners is burned by a service provider, one of two results (or both) can occur. The owner becomes distrustful of that vendor's whole industry, or the owner becomes distrustful of anyone else s/he has to rely on to get business done right.

  By putting down your competition, you are feeding that distrust of your industry. Ultimately, you are telling the cynical business owner that you and your company are the same as their old vendor. You're informing them that their cynicism is justified, which only makes your road more difficult to travel with this client.

- **Maintain neutrality in regard to your competition.** Have no reaction when you find out who the old provider is, except to acknowledge the information. Offer no opinions. Your opinion doesn't matter on this topic ... certainly not during the interview process or the introductory work process. If you're told who the old provider was, then use it solely for information—you should know the company's reputation, you should know the services they provide, and you should know how they bill clients. If you don't, then this is a great opportunity to find out.

- **Be fair.** I remember the first few times I took over a client from another IT consulting company. I was horrified for the client to see all the mistakes, missteps, or lack of effort on the IT vendor's part. There were so many action items for me to work through. I really felt bad for the client. I blamed the IT vendor. Did they not know what they were doing? However, after nearly a decade of providing this service to both commercial and residential clients, I learned that there are as many different factors for each client as there are cities in the United States (give or take). I learned, first hand, how difficult it is to handle so many different industries, personalities, tasks, and services. I learned the complexities of balancing home and work responsibilities. I learned how hard it is to work with little or no sleep some days.

Most importantly, I learned not to judge the other IT vendors. No one is perfect. While there are some people who shouldn't own businesses or who don't try very hard at perfecting their craft, most everyone is trying very hard to do a good job, to fight against the everyday struggles, stresses, and demands. It's not my job to judge.

I learned I could be judged just as easily as the last guy. As a consultant, my job was to find action items to correct. I did that well. At any given moment, another consultant could come behind me and find items I may have missed or work done differently than how they'd do it. A consultant's job is to consult. That's what they do. So, I felt it didn't do any IT vendor (or the industry) any good to waste time being unfair to the work, workers, or processes because my work, my processes, and I could be judged just as easily.

- **Listen.** The client will tell you what they want. You just have to listen. Most of the time without having to ask too many questions. People like to talk about themselves or other things that are important to them. Their business is important to them. Most will talk about it to no end, so just get them talking. They'll tell you everything you need to know about them, their business practices, their old vendor, and so on.

Listening to their opinion of themselves is important because it gives you a feel for how working with them will be. Will they be easygoing? Demanding? Rude?

Listening to their business practices allows you to hear, for example, how they work, what's important on a daily basis, and what the most critical part of their business processes is. Listening to them talk about their old vendor gives you a front row seat to their expectations (and coincidentally the things you have to do to build the relationship and keep their business). Some examples from my experience are:

- "The old vendor invoiced me every month, but there was no information on the invoice about the work they performed that month." MY ACTION: Detail work performed.
- "I paid for data backups, but I never found out how to get the data if I needed it." MY ACTION: Detail processes for client.
- "I gave the old vendor a key to the business doors, so he could come and go and work around my busy schedule. He developed a drug problem, and I had to change all the locks." MY ACTION: Don't do drugs. Don't accept keys to client's businesses.
- The client paid the vendor for parts up front. The vendor never purchased the parts and didn't ever call the client again. MY ACTION: Always be honest.

Seriously, if you listen, you will find out EVERYTHING!

Additionally, most of the time all clients want is

communication. These are people who probably control every aspect of their business, except the aspects they've learned they shouldn't control. They export that job to someone else (you/your company), which probably causes them anxiety. Figure out how to ease that anxiety by listening to them. The result will be a better relationship between you and the client.

- **Focus on the positive differences between you and your competition.** As mentioned earlier, you should know who your competition is. If you don't know, then you have the opportunity to research them. Most clients aren't looking for your opinion on their old service provider (*they already have one, which is why they are talking to you*), so don't offer one. Just offer the positive differences.
    - If your fees are less than the old provider's, then spotlight that information.
    - If your services are more focused on this client's industry, spotlight that.
    - If your range of provided services is broader than your competition's, spotlight that.

  Just don't talk bad about the competition. It will negatively reflect on you and your character.

- **Realize the limitations you see in your competition's work may have been enacted by the client.** You've gathered a list of action items the last vendor didn't do. You've decided the client was being taken advantage of because they were being billed for items that were never completed. You've decided the old service provider hired nothing but hacks, truly terrible technicians. Did they? What are the other factors of this equation?

A consultant's job is to consult, to find things wrong that need to be fixed. Yes.

But, it's not a consultant's job to approve the work that gets performed. The client decides that. The client pays for that. If the client doesn't think something is important, then they'll say no. If the client has a limited budget, then only the most affordably pressing action items will be completed.

This is another reason to not judge the old service provider. The client could have halted progress.

This Should Be Obvious

§

All of what I'm writing in this book I have experienced in one way or another, so I know these situations do arise. I like to think I was able to navigate through them successfully, but I know there are people out there who wouldn't and didn't; and, yet, many others who have never had these things happen to them. Maybe they wouldn't even know how to handle them, if they did happen. By reading about these situations here, maybe you or your staff will figure out (or can discuss) how to handle them before troubles arise. That's the hope.

Bedroom time. This is when being a professional is really important. As an IT consultant for home users, I've worked on TVs, computers, laptops, tablets, and wireless devices, to name a few devices. Home users store these devices throughout their house. Oftentimes some or all of them are stored in the users' bedroom. As I've documented numerous times in this book I work with many female clients in their homes. When you're working in a bedroom with a woman, it is extra important to be professional. They are leading you into the most private room of their home. This takes a high level of trust and vulnerability for a woman to do. It also takes a great amount of professionalism, trust, and vulnerability for you, as the male technician. (I am telling this from the female client/male technician point of view, but I imagine it's somewhat similar in reverse.) A worst case scenario could be that the female client mistakes one of your comments or movements while in the bedroom and reports to your manager (or the police) your inappropriateness.

To avoid mistaken perceptions, incorporate these best practices:

- Maintain a safe distance from the female client without being obvious. When not in use, keep your hands interlocked together in front of you or behind your back.
- Don't sit or lie on the bed with or without the client present.
- Without fail, maintain your "Yes, ma'am" manners. Maintain your utmost politeness.
- Take the equipment from the room to work in a less private area, like the kitchen or living room, if possible.
- If left alone, then maintain the highest ethical standards possible. Do not look around or inside anything.

Shower time. Often I'd find myself meeting a female client at her home based on her workout schedule. She'd invite me into the home, show me the problems she was experiencing, and then she'd retreat to her bedroom for a shower. She'd often have somewhere else to go and wanted me to fix the problem in between her workout time and her next appointment. This is the understanding here: Just because your client is taking a shower while you are working inside her home doesn't mean she is inviting you into her bathroom to join her. *(NOTE: I did not learn this the hard way, by the way.)*

Seriously, this should be obvious.

What I think it actually means is that through your previous interaction with her, she has deemed you highly professional, responsible, and trustworthy to a supreme degree. It's a compliment. Don't say or do anything to the contrary of what your female client has decided about you.

From the business owner's point of view, things like this are terribly nerve-racking. They are sending out technicians to people's homes and offices, where any situation can arise. What a liability! There is no training in the world to prepare a technician for each situation. However, what the business owner hopes to do, and what this book hopes to do, is set up some general, professional rules of behavior that can be maintained in any circumstance. These rules keep you, your company, and your business owner safe when these situations do arise.

Interpersonal Skills: Communication

Verbal Pause + Casual Responses = You Lose

§

Within our collective communication behaviors, one of the hardest tasks for a person to undertake is eliminating the use of "um" and other verbal pauses from their vocabulary. Doing so goes against all that's, unfortunately, become natural to many people's communication practices. I know I struggle to overcome this problem.

Using these verbal pauses, as well as casual responses in professional conversation, creates a less than professional appearance and presentation. It makes it seem as though you don't know what you're talking about, you're making up the answer, or you didn't take an English class. Additionally, it can become very distracting for the listener.

As I listen to a presentation, the biggest distraction for me is the use of the word "like." It distracts me to no end. Not the use of it one time, but the use of it in every sentence. Once I'm, like, distracted, the presenter loses me, like, completely. I never find my way back to, like, hearing the presenter's message. You know, like, what I am doing? I'm counting the times I hear "like," and, I know I'm, like, not the only one in the audience who this, like, impacts.

The same is true of interpersonal communication, when you're talking with a client face to face. After the 20th "um" or "like," they're gone. By using those verbal pauses, you create distance between you and your client. When a client pays a professional, they want professionalism. Verbal pauses, as described here, are not professional.

Casual responses are also losers in the communication game. Words like: nope, yeah, yep, uh-huh, huh, and so on. Don't ask, "Huh?" NOT PROFESSIONAL. Say, "Excuse me?" Or, "I'm sorry; I didn't hear what you said. Will you repeat that?" PROFESSIONAL.

Remember, the goal is to present yourself in a professional, human manner. That means provide premier respect (service) to your client while maintaining your personality. Your job is to find simple ways to display genuinely that respect. "Huh?" doesn't elevate you toward that goal.

Here are some ways to keep the verbal pauses and the casual responses at bay when you're communicating with a client (or giving a presentation):

Know the subject matter. The best antidote when communicating with a client is to know your stuff! We lose sight of our overall communication goals when we are stumbling to answer questions to which we don't know the answers. So, don't wing it. Know what you're talking about *before* you begin the conversation. Think of possible questions the client might ask prior to starting the conversation. Have answers ready.

Slow down your mental thoughts. Breathe! Professional conversations shouldn't proceed at the same rate of speed as does a friendly conversation. Professional conversations are more limited in scope and should be approached methodically. Slow down. Think before you respond. I was recently on a call. I was nervous. As I answered the first question, I realized I hadn't taken a breath before I answered it. I was just rambling on. I quickly balanced myself. I took a deep breath and exhaled slowly. I reminded myself I was only speaking to a person. There was no reason to be nervous. By the end of the exhale, I had relaxed. Doing so fixed the situation this time. The rest of the conversation went as I had hoped it would—positively, professionally, and successfully.

If you don't know something, say so. Look, providing an answer that satisfies another human being's curiosity is empowering. Believe me. But no one, no matter the expectation, can know everything. It's better to give the right information than to make something up. If you're asked a question you don't know the answer to, then just say "I don't know off the top of my head. I'll look it up and call you with the information I find." Then look it up AND call the client with the answer. Not knowing something also humanizes you to the client. It makes them a little more comfortable around you. But more importantly, you're being honest, which shows your genuineness. That will earn you many points with your client.

When communicating, just remember:

- Be honest.
- Be genuine.
- Think about the words coming out of your mouth in order to eliminate verbal pauses and casual responses.
- Present yourself professionally.

Wash Your Mouth With Soap

§

This one is simple. No cursing. It's low class.

What words do you want people to utilize when describing you as a professional? Are these the same things you think about your own work product?

- Very intelligent?
- Excellent communicator?
- Hard worker?
- Meets deadlines?
- Flexible?
- Resourceful?
- Reliable?

When you curse in professional settings, you change what people think of you. Usually the thinking is changed negatively.

- Intelligent. Cursing is almost always associated with the opposite of intelligence.
- Communicator. "He can't find a better adjective than 'shitty'?"
- Hard worker. "He sure works hard to include so many four-letter words."
- Deadline. "The closer the deadline got, the more vulgar words she used."
- Flexible. "She sure was flexible with her use of the F-bomb."
- Resourceful. "She resourcefully came up with new ways

to use bad words."

- Reliable. "You sure can rely on him to use foul language."

There's just no need to use it in a professional environment.

For your clients who don't use that language, they will cringe when you do, which will distract them from your message.

For your clients who do use that language, they won't care if you don't use it.

If you're the owner of the business or the decision-maker, implement a policy stating very clearly that foul language should never be used when associating with clients or potential clients … even if the client curses.

Sexy Talk

§

Pick up any company's Human Resources guidelines, there is some mention of sexual harassment. Sometimes that "mention" is a few pages long. Most small and medium businesses don't have HR guidelines or even a guide on policies and procedures for that matter. They should. Even if the only staff member is the owner, there should be some outline/idea on the acceptable ways to communicate with clients.

In this world of networking, of building relationships that extend beyond the conference room, and of the casualness and openness of conversation via social media, it's hard to know where the line between appropriate-and-inappropriate and casual-and-professional connection is drawn.

That's why knowing your clients is important. Some clients would not object to a sexual innuendo or two. Some would run you out of their office with a pitchfork, if you used one.

The best advice is to not discuss, even in a joking fashion, sex at all with clients ... even if there is an attraction on both sides of the conversation.

When in doubt, don't use innuendo-laden language. The relationship in which you are attempting to use sexually suggestive language must have extended beyond professional boundaries in some way. Hold your tongue. Think about the goals of your relationship with this client. Do they align with sexually suggestive comments? Consider why you're slipping from professional conversation to casual conversation. Are or could there be negative repercussions because of these comments? Where do you want this relationship to go? Does that match your personal and professional selves? The answers you'll find probably will point you in a direction away from using sexually suggestive comments.

Put simply, if you ever doubt something, don't do it. Where there is doubt, there's a reason for the doubt. Listen to it. In this scenario, if you doubt the acceptance of a sexually suggestive comment, don't express it.

There are other fish in the sea. Listen, the female client you are interested in may be beautiful, funny, and smart. She may be all the things you want from a woman. Same situation for the man of your dreams. Both are clients. Both are business relationships. It's hard to put food on the table. Don't risk your professional integrity (sales numbers, reputation, and service level, for example) with an attraction. There are other attractive, funny, and smart people in the world.

Professional topics don't include sexuality, unless you're a sex therapist. If you are a computer consultant whose job it is to provide word processing solutions to clients, then there is no need to discuss anything of a sexual nature. If you are a cable installer, then there is no need to discuss anything of a sexual nature. If you are an accountant, then there is no need to discuss anything of a sexual nature. If you are a plumber, there is no need to discuss anything of a sexual nature (despite the obvious temptation to employ "pipe" jokes). If you are a taxidermist, there is no need to discuss anything of a sexual nature. You see where I'm going with this? There is no need in a professional conversation to discuss anything in a sexual nature … unless you're a sex therapist.

Interpersonal Skills: Networking

Socializing With Clients

§

The beauty of having clients is that you've built a relationship with them, and so much goodness can come from these relationships. However, balancing the fine-line between personal and professional is often complicated and confusing. If you can balance it correctly, these relationships will endure, and that's the goal. Maintaining relationships means you're maintaining continual income through the years. This helps your business maintain, grow, and flourish.

While building and maintaining these relationships, some people lose track of the line between personal and professional. This is where people get into trouble. They can hurt themselves, their families, their business, and even their respective industries by crossing the line. Infidelity can destroy marriages and families. Inappropriate information exchange can ruin deals, taint studies, and even bring down political careers.

Some companies and industries have policies against this type of fraternization, but even with these guidelines people still end up on the wrong side of the line. The problem is that you must connect with people to make them clients, but you can't get too close.

This is a set of ideas that may help in this balancing act:

- **Know yourself.** Are you susceptible to crossing the line, to losing sight of the line? If you are, search yourself. Figure out why you are susceptible and work to repair that part of you.
- **While connecting with a client, leave out the truly personal**

information. Don't complain about your marriage or spouse. Don't delve too deeply into the problems you have with your children, parents, money, etc. That is your private life, not your professional life. These clients are your professional connections. For example, when I was divorcing, I told certain clients of the impending dissolution of marriage. However, I didn't tell them the gritty details of why the divorce was happening. That wasn't any of their business. I felt they had a right to know why my typical service level had decreased. They understood the boundaries of our relationship and never asked what happened in the marriage. That is a good example of a professional relationship.

- **Going to dinners, drinks, etc. alone with the opposite sex can be a bad idea.** Drinks lead to lower inhibitions. Lower inhibitions lead to breaking of each of these rules.

Other inappropriate behavior that falls below the level of professionalism can impact your work life, depending on your industry regulations, your company regulations, and your team atmosphere. So, here are some simple rules to aid you through the relationship:

- **Remember, some clients are only friendly with you because you have something to offer them.** They need your services. They know, as you do, if you build a relationship, corners can be cut. Sometimes those corners are processes that bog down progress and sometimes they are billable hours. Perhaps they can get you to knock off a couple hours here and there.

- **Don't confide in your clients about your company's financial situation.** For example, you might confide that the company is doing great, making more money than the last few years put together. If your client is only there because he is working the relationship (rather than being a real friend who would be happy for you), then he may start slowing down his payments to you. Rather than paying your invoice in two weeks, it changes to every four weeks. Then perhaps it slows to every six or eight weeks. "He's doing fine," he might tell himself. "He'll be OK if I just wait a little longer to pay him." On the other hand, you tell a client you are really struggling, be it financially or to complete all of your work. Your client might jump ship, wanting to partner with a stronger vendor who isn't going to go out of business or who can provide faster service. This could really impact your business negatively.

Again, it's hard to know who is a real friend and who is a client-friend.

- **So, if s/he's a client-friend, then s/he's not your real friend.** Be honest with yourself—if you sold your business, would the relationship endure? If you were fired or changed jobs, would the relationship endure?

- **If you were friends before s/he was your client, then confiding is all right, as it is part of the pre-existing relationship.** However, I'd still caution you, when doing business with friends. Depending on your business industry and what service you provide for your clients, this situation can become a war zone if mismanaged.

- **Don't tell a client the corner you cut on another client's project.** They will immediately start wondering what corner(s) you cut on their projects.

These are certainly cynical viewpoints, but they do happen. And the results are real life consequences for you, your company, and your family, so keep your cards close to your vest and remember there is a line between your real life and your professional life you shouldn't cross.

Networking Spiderwebs

§

There are a great number of people who believe in doing business on the golf course. I know deals are still closed there, but they are also getting done in more and more places. Perhaps because of organizations' need to create value for their members, there are a growing number of events specifically built for the sole purpose of networking. Those who attend these events know they are there for one reason and one reason only: to expose their name, company, and services to as many people as possible at one time.

The local Chamber of Commerce probably holds the majority of these events; however, there are leads groups locally organized or franchised as well. These groups get together before work, for lunch, and/or after work. At these meetings or events, there may be presentations or lectures that occur, refreshments served, and/or happy hour drinks on hand. I won't go into more detail about these kinds of groups because that's not what I am writing about. What's important for this book is how to build relationships in these settings, so I'll focus on that instead of how these various meetings are organized.

Embrace your adventurous side. Many people are afraid of these networking events. The thought of talking to new people can be scary. Often people are afraid of rejection. Perhaps they are introverts or maybe they feel they don't have anything interesting to say; that they'd rather do their job than tell people about it. Those are normal reactions. Although, if you're in business for yourself or trying to position yourself in a salesperson position within your company, then you have to go to and participate in these events. You have to meet new people. Just keep telling yourself it's fun and interesting. You might one day believe it and have fun meeting interesting people.

Where else can you meet so many other like-minded people? If you are a business owner and you're at one of these events, guess who most of the other people at the event will be? Business owners. If you're a salesperson, then there will be other sales people there as well. This is their hunting ground, and it's their hunting ground for a reason: it works. Introduce yourself to someone and ask what they do. If they're wearing a name tag, then use it. Just say, "Hi, _____."

Remember, you're not the only one there selling. They're selling too, which means they are eager to talk to people just like you. The person you meet could change your life. Maybe they hire you. Maybe they introduce you to someone else, who in turn hires you. Maybe you change their lives with the many wonderful offerings you have professionally and personally. You never know unless you say hello.

Take your business cards. Whatever you do, don't forget your business cards. As archaic as it sounds, business cards are still handed out in the pound-full at these events. How else will you remember whom to contact if you want to hire them? Market to them? Go to lunch with them? And, how else will they remember you? I'm sure you're a memorable person, but are you memorable enough that everyone you talk to will remember your name, your company name, the physical address, P.O. Box number, the company tagline, your email, office phone number, FAX number, and your cell phone? Probably not.

While distributing the cards is important, don't be the guy that rushes through the crowd without speaking to anyone, forcing your business cards onto whoever is in your path. This never works. People really do want to do business with people they know and like. They won't get to know you if you thrust your cards into their hands as you run by them.

Dress nicely. Depending on the theme of the event, look the part. If it's a business event, then wear your best uniform or your nicest slacks and dress shirt. If it's a Western themed event, wear cowboy boots, and a cowboy hat, for example. Remember, you can always arrive dressed too "up," but you never want to arrive dressed too "down." Look like a success, no matter what you wear. Strive to reflect the people you want to do business with.

Watch your mouth. One key to success is being respectable, ethical, and responsible. One of the easiest ways to present this during a networking function is to not utilize unsavory language. You'll present yourself as vulgar or crass, and no one will want to call you. Be calm, pleasant, jovial, and respectful to others. If you reflect who you want to be, then that's how people will see you.

Chew your food. For God's sake, don't talk with your mouth full of food! What's wrong with you? The last thing you need to do is spit food on someone to whom you're talking.

Employ eating manners. If you're having a breakfast meeting and all they are serving is muffins, don't take a huge bite out of the muffin, like you would an apple. Break a piece off and eat it in small bites. If there is fruit, then eat that. It shows you're health conscious, which demonstrates to people your respect for your own body, which in turn shows how you'll treat other people and the work they entrust to you—with respect. Plus, it's easily manipulated with a fork and you can limit how much goes in your mouth at one time.

At lunch, skip the hamburger and order the salmon. Eating food with your hands during a business lunch is not smart. The burger will be messy to eat, as you literally jam it in your mouth. Pick salmon, chicken breast, a salad, or something like that. They are easy to eat with cutlery, chew, and swallow.

For events after work, finger foods are common—meatballs, chicken wings or tenders, or slider sandwiches. At events like this, if possible, I will grab a plate and make off to an isolated corner. I'll quickly eat alone (not enough to fill me up but enough to keep me from feeling hungry) and then return to the event.

All in all, though, go with the flow. If your business is hamburger meat and you're attending a function where the only thing to eat is hamburger, then have a hamburger. Heck, throw on some cheese and chow down. Still, be watchful of how you're eating. You don't want to look like a manner-less Neanderthal.

Don't drink too much. No anecdote here. Simply don't drink too much. If you get drunk at one of these events, then you'll always be *that* guy. You can't come across as respectful and professional if you are slurring your words. Save it for home or the weekends with your buddies. Never at a business function.

Talk about you. Yes, you have to tell the people you meet about your work. That's why you're at this networking event after all. They need to know your industry, your reputation, and possibly who you know in common. But, they don't need to *only* hear that. People can hire whoever they want. They can find dozens of companies who offer the same services. Why should they hire you? Because of *you*, that's why. Get beyond the business talk and let them get to know you. Let them learn something about you that they can remember for the next time you see or speak to them.

Talk about them. This is vital. Charismatic people don't talk about themselves. They let the other people talk. Charismatic people react to what others are saying. They ask questions. They are genuinely interested in other people. In helping other people. In knowing other people. So be charismatic! Learn everything you can about the person. Really pay attention! This is a great time to figure out if you want to work with this person, whose guard is down because your charisma has put them at ease. Perhaps they aren't being professional. You can really get a feel for how this person will be to work with. If you don't like what you're seeing, politely move along. If you like what you're seeing, then learn more. Build a relationship. After you see them a couple more times, you just might get that business call or referral.

Early and good bye. Show up early, leave early. That way you see everyone twice. This is a favorite practice of mine. Not many people are ever present before or as the event is starting, so you should be. You have more time to mingle with only the few people who are there. It's good quality time. Fresh time; they aren't worn down by "being on" the whole time. They haven't even started "being on."

As more people arrive, you can see them and greet them. You get full exposure to the people arriving. It's the best way to see everyone to whom you hope to speak.

Leaving early works best for after work events. The announcement reads 5:30 PM to 7:30 PM, but people always end up sticking around. I like leaving, in this example, at 7 PM. As you make your way through the crowd again, you get to see the majority of the people whom you've already spoken with. You get a second opportunity to talk to them and say good bye. It shows manners, and it's an easy way to get a second face-to-face with them.

Follow-up within a couple days. It's always a great sales tactic to follow-up via, at least, email with the people you meet. I recommend you do, but don't sell to them. Instead, send a nice message about being happy to have met them. Maybe include a quick quip about the event where you met and then close the email cordially. Make sure your web site and phone number are included in your email signature. If they're interested in your services today, they'll check out your web site. If not today, then they have your information in business card format and in their email for future reference.

Remember, this follow-up message should reinforce your charisma and likeability, as well as the building of trust and respect. It's not about getting a sales call meeting. Be patient. It'll come; when it does, you'll be in a much better position to close the deal because you'll know the person really wants to do business with *you*.

Interpersonal Skills: Endings

Funerals

§

If you're in business for any real length of time, you will have clientele or their family members pass away. If you have used the principles and philosophies within this book to develop genuine and authentic relationships with clients, then these life events will certainly impact you in some way. Too many possible ways to mention here beyond this one: people you care for professionally, socially, and/or personally are hurting.

There are no hard and fast rules in this situation, but it's appropriate to choose one or more of these options:

- Mailing a sympathy card
- Attending the funeral and other services
- Send flowers or donate to a non-profit in lieu of flowers

Of course, the option you choose depends on your level of connectedness to the client, so you will have to decipher which option or combination of options matches your personality and relationship. But, you should choose one of these above options.

The opposite side of this coin is when someone in your life passes. If you have a good relationship with some of your clients, they will mail you cards, come to the funeral, or send flowers.

Despite your pain, if you're able to muster the strength, then try to thank each one of those clients for coming. These are people you wouldn't expect or think would come. It's a gift to you that they came. Your "thank you" provided to them will only connect them to you in a greater, deeper way. It shows your level of commitment to them that you would make the time to thank them personally. However, if you're unable to thank them personally, that's all right too. They'll understand, but the next time you see them don't forget to thank them.

I have recently, unfortunately, attended two funerals related to my clients. One was a funeral for the sister of one of my clients. I had met her a couple times and spoken to her numerous times on the phone, as I had done with this client's parents and other two siblings, too. During the services, I expected in no way, and sought out in no way, to interact with my client. He saw me, smiled, and waved. He knew I was there. That was enough for me. I wanted to support him and his family during their loss. I felt I had accomplished this desire, just by him knowing I was present. Thirty minutes after the funeral, this client called me to personally thank me for attending. It was such a classy, wonderfully polite thing for him to do during that time of personal loss. I couldn't believe it, and I still think amazingly warm thoughts about that moment, his class, and his strength.

Another funeral I attended was of a client who passed away unexpectedly. I had connected with him on a personal level through the six years we worked together. We met occasionally for a drink to discuss life, business, religion, marriage, and personal growth. I treasured the time he took out of his life and business to be a self-appointed mentor to me. His wife stopped me on the way into the funeral and thanked me for providing her husband friendship and service.

In both cases, I went to support other people but instead received comfort from them, which is what funerals and community are all about—a collective healing. If you have clients, then you have relationships. Attending these functions are helpful to everyone related to the situation, including yourself.

Notes

§

Before delving into the next ideas, methods, philosophies, principles, and best practices, examine again each of the Core Principles again. Write down any ideas of your own in relation to the ideas presented here. How do they apply to your job? To your client interactions? Do you agree or disagree with the principles presented? Use this examination as a conversation started, either with your staff or your manager or your business's owner.

Part Six: Thank You

Say "Thank You" Often

§

Other than doing an exceptional job resolving a client's problems, this is the best way to get a second call from the client: say thank you.

A practice that seems to be disappearing is sending "Thank you" notes. Hand-written "Thank you" notes. They are just as important at the start of a relationship as they are in the middle and at the end. You just have to take a few minutes to write them out.

These personalized notes open the door to a client's appreciation for your efforts. Appreciation is a warm emotion. When that's felt, thoughts of you are associated in your client's mind with warmth, comfort, and goodness. That's a great first step for building a relationship.

When a thank you letter is sent to a client during an ongoing relationship, you remind the client of your appreciation for their business and of their interactions with you. Remember, once these client relationships are established, these are the people paying you so you can put food on your family's table. Even though you're earning that pay by providing a service to these clients, don't you think they deserve your respect and appreciation? Don't you want to continue that trend of putting food on your family' table? Simply doing a great job isn't enough.

Finally, at the end of a relationship (say you sell your business), a "Thank You" note lets your long-time clients know that you appreciate their long-standing trust in you as a service provider. Additionally, it is your final declaration of goodwill toward your clients. Unless you're retiring and moving to Costa Rica, you will most likely see these people again, perhaps, at church or a restaurant. Don't you want them to think nicely of you and say hello when they see you? You do, if you had built a relationship with them. Plus, if you're not retiring and moving away, then you'll start another business or work for another company. Leave your long-standing clients with warm appreciation and fondness of you, and maybe they'll move with you to your new venture.

On a simpler notation, it's just good manners to thank the people who have supported you, believed in you and your skills, and helped you support your family.

That being said:

"Thank you for reading. I hope at least a few chapters aided you in your business (and even your personal) life. Remember that your clients are human and they need you to be human too. Fight for them, be honest, care about them, relate to them, and complete your work in an exceptional fashion; most of them will stick with you for a very long time."

Notes

§

Write down any of your overall ideas of your own in relation to the ideas presented here. How do they apply to your job? To your client interactions? Do you agree or disagree with the principles presented? Use this examination as a conversation started, either with your staff or your manager or your business's owner.

_____

_____

_____

_____

_____

_____

_____

_____

_____

_____

_____

_____

About The Author

§

Chris Wendel is a native of Lakeland, Florida. He attended the University of South Florida and graduated with a degree in English/Technical Writing. He later returned to university and earned a degree in Computer Network Administration. Chris owned and operated an IT consulting company in Florida for almost a decade before working as a Relationship Manager for a global company.

He is an Amazon.com bestselling author for his short story, *Human After All: The Pen Pal Chronicle*. The short story chronicles the teen years of the villain in his debut novel, *Human After All*, which introduced characters Det. Tom Gray and Valerie Hardy. In the novel, the characters battle an evil villain who makes them face the fears which have halted their lives. The follow-up novel, *King of Pain*, featuring Det. Tom Gray will be released at the end of 2013. In the summer of 2013, Chris's book of poems, *Unfinished*, will be available.

There is an accompanying book to *Converting Customers to Clients*. *On Strengthening Business Relationships* is a book of standalone business quotes.

He is currently available for book club engagements, organizational presentations for both his creative writing and client relationship/customer service topics. He blogs at his web site cwendel.com about various topics, which include arts and entertainment, business, customer service, writing, music, parenting, and more.

Chris is involved in numerous community activities and groups, like Kiwanis and the local futbol club. Chris enjoys football, soccer, music, stories and reading, as well as spending precious time with friends and family.

cwendel.com
Facebook | Twitter | Instagram | Tumblr | Flickr

Get the accompanying book!

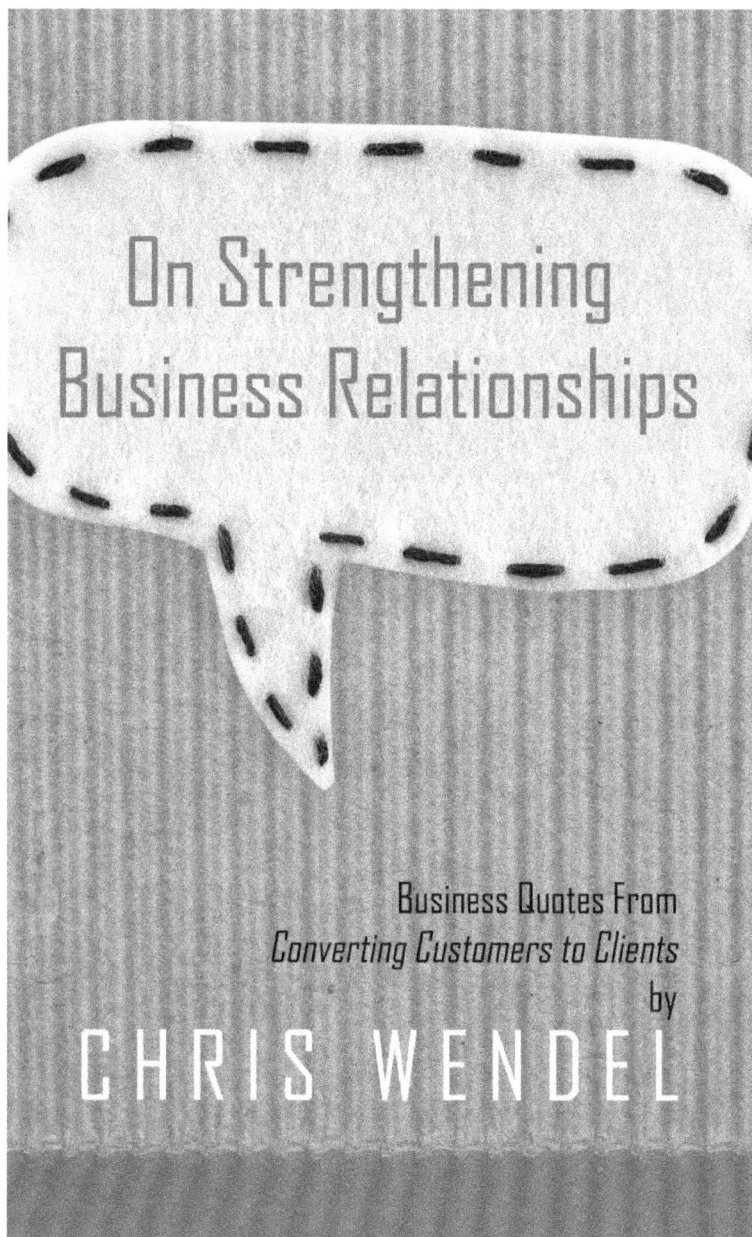

On Strengthening Business Relationships

Business Quotes From
Converting Customers to Clients
by
CHRIS WENDEL